A Kist
Thistles

An anthology of radical poetry from contemporary Scotland

Edited by Jim Aitken

with images by Fiona Stewart

'The function, as it seems to me,
O' Poetry is to bring to be
At lang, lang last that unity...'

—Hugh MacDiarmid, *A Drunk Man Looks at the Thistle*

First published 2020 by **Culture Matters.**
Culture Matters promotes a socialist and progressive approach to art, culture and politics. See www.culturematters.org.uk

Copyright © the contributors
Cover image: Fiona Stewart
Commissioning Editor: Mike Quille
Layout and typesetting: Alan Morrison
ISBN 978-1-912710-32-4

Culture Matters is grateful to Unite Community in Scotland, and University and College Union in Scotland, for their support for this anthology

Contents

ABROAD

ELSEWHERE

Introduction—Taking the Long View

By Jim Aitken

The position of Scottish Makar was instituted in 2004 by the Scottish Parliament. The title harked back to a time when poets were given their full place in Scottish society to speak for the nation—and just to speak. That was before Union and before the Reformation. These 'auld makars', as Edwin Morgan called them, *'tickled a Scottish king's ear with melody and ribaldry and frank advice.'* The names of Barbour, Blind Harry, Henryson, Dunbar and Douglas are all conjured up in this comment.

Let's start with Morgan, appointed Makar in 2004. He was asked to write a poem for the official opening of the new Scottish Parliament building at Holyrood on 9 October 2004. His opening line implored *'light of the mind, shine out!'* In the rest of the poem he plays the part of Makar in full by saying what he does not want from the Scottish Parliament:

A nest of fearties is what we do not want.
A symposium of procrastinators is what we do not want.
A phalanx of forelock-tuggers is what we do not want.

What he does want from the Scottish Parliament is for it *'to be filled with thinking persons.'* Because of illness Morgan's poem was read by Liz Lochhead, who became Scotland's second official Makar. Her own poem was read there on July 1st 2011 and it looked back to Morgan's theme of a Parliament that is 'open'. Lochhead's poem was actually called 'Open.' She sought for those elected to this Parliament to *'Open your minds—to change.'* She called for the Parliament to *'let the people petition to be heard.'* She called for *'Open-ness'* and for *'Integrity, Compassion, Justice and Wisdom.'*

Scotland's third Makar is Jackie Kay and in her poem 'The Long View', read to the Parliament for its 20th anniversary on 29 June 2019, there was a sense that Scotland had changed as a nation. She acknowledged that a great deal of hard campaigning had gone into Scotland winning back her Parliament, and seemed to sum up this sense particularly well saying that the Parliament's existence is *'a process, not an event.'* It is this Parliament, she said, that *'is about who we are, how we carry ourselves'* as a nation.

As a gay woman of colour and of Scottish-Nigerian descent, pride in being Scottish is testimony to how far Scotland has travelled. In her poem she can proudly say of the Parliament *'the door's open and I've come ben this bonny chamber.'* That is a sign that real progress has been made. For her *'twenty years on my country has changed'* but there is still further to go because she says *'we're taking the long view.'* Scotland is in no way a finished project.

What these three poems have in common is an optimism, but an optimism that is firmly rooted in the ordinary people of Scotland. All three poets are speaking for the people. There is nothing remotely platitudinous or posturing in any way to the Parliament. These poems are in fact holding the Parliament to account. This makes them radical poems, yet they all seem normal and natural.

And that is what being radical is all about. It is about trying to challenge what is wrong in society and in the world at large and making everything somehow normal—as it actually should be. Society and the world are how they have been made by those in power. Poets who wish to challenge inequality, injustice, discrimination, abuse of power, class division, war and ignorance do so not for themselves but for the myriad of others suffering such iniquities. Given the state of the world, radicalism is normal and natural; it is the response to all the things that are wrong. In our world today it is impossible not to be radical assuming that as 'thinking persons' our conscience and sense of morality can still be aroused despite 24 hour TV. Maybe that is why there are so many writers in jail, and why so many journalists are killed.

A Kist of Thistles brings together 62 Scottish writers who all have something radical yet something normal to say. Many take a position on Scotland's 'long view'. When I was asked to edit this anthology by Mike Quille of **Culture Matters**, I recall saying to him that we may get an inordinate number of poems on Scottish independence. And indeed they are here, in their own distinctive voices. There are shades of opinion, and that is a cause for celebration because it implies an engagement with current Scottish politics. Yet these poems take up only part of this anthology.

The poets in the anthology show that they are internationally aware, environmentally aware and concerned for those being treated unjustly and unfairly. There are no poems here in favour of war, inequality and the continuation of class division, and that is because the poets here have at heart their concern for ordinary people. The polar opposite to such radicalism is the reactionary viewpoint that wants to hold back all normal demands for progressive change and the people who fall into this camp are called—among other things—conservatives. Their philosophy can be summed up in the unholy trinity of 'Me, Myself, I.'

Poetry of the people

In 1951 Edwin Muir was Warden of Newbattle Abbey College and he gave a lecture there saying that what distinguished Scottish from English poetry was that the former was mainly a poetry of the people, not of a class. One of the main themes in Scottish poetry, claimed Muir, was liberty.

This year is the 700th anniversary of the Declaration of Arbroath when Pope John XXII was petitioned to accept Scotland as an independent and sovereign nation. The fact that Scottish PEN have launched their own publication *Declarations* to mark this significant event, and the Federation of Writers (Scotland) are doing something similar, shows exactly the kind of engaged debate that is going on within Scotland's literary community and within the nation at large. Liberty remains a key theme of our writers precisely because it shows concern for the people.

When the rich and powerful speak of 'liberty' and 'freedom' they are actually speaking about the freedom to plunder, exploit, expropriate and amass as much as they can, however they can. This is why there is warfare, climate change, pollution and scarcity. *A Kist of Thistles* addresses much of this.

Morgan, Lochhead and Kay all challenge the Scottish Parliament to be what it was worth fighting for. Poets are often ahead of the political game and it is the poets that are invariably worth listening to rather than the politicians. Shelley, in his 'Defence of Poetry' in 1821, called poets *'the unacknowledged legislators of the world.'*

I am proud that we have Makars to say what they think and write what they think. The Holyrood Parliament, by allowing its poets to address it in the way that it does, makes the Westminster Parliament reveal itself as something far less open. It is a Parliament drowning itself in arcane traditions and pomposity as much as pomp. These last 20 or so years have shown not only how far Scotland has come but how far she may yet travel. When the House of Commons allows Benjamin Zephaniah or Roger Robinson to address it with a poem pleading with it to deal with its history of slavery, imperialism and racism, that would show an acceptance that things have to change. Until then we are left with Black Rod or Jackie Kay, and I know who I prefer.

Gaelic

This anthology features all Scotland's languages—Gaelic, Scots and English. I am particularly delighted that the anthology has managed to feature the work of three Gaelic poets. In one poem by Anne Frater 'Dìomhanas/Futility', she writes movingly about heather—about its fragility, its funding and neglect. The poem can be read on another level, with the heather as metaphor for Gaelic culture and language itself.

Gaelic has a history of neglect long before the Reformation and Union. Many historians see the reign of Malcolm III as the beginning of the language's decline. His wife was Margaret of Wessex—later canonised as St Margaret—who brought with her to Scotland her English bishops and monks, and her English tongue that she wished the rest of us to follow.

There is also a wonderful geographical spread in this anthology. There are writers from Shetland and Orkney, Lewis, Harris and Skye, the Highlands, Aberdeen, Dundee and Angus, Fife, Edinburgh, Glasgow and the west of Scotland, the Borders, the Scottish outpost of Nova Scotia, two Scots writers based in England, another in Northern Ireland, and one in Finland. With the geographical spread and the linguistic diversity on display this anthology is truly representative of contemporary Scotland.

Scots

The use of Scots was certainly considered inferior and uncouth with the advent of Union. It had actually been under attack after the Union of the Crowns in 1603, but political Union hastened this further. Scotland's great Enlightenment luminaries like David Hume and Adam Smith abhorred Scotticisms, saw themselves as providing the intellectual basis for the Union, and seemed content to call themselves North Britons. Of course, those to the south had no inclination to call themselves Southern Britons. They were and are English though the term 'Britain' is often invoked to bring the Celtic components of this entity into line.

Scottish school children had their Scots belted out of them. Scots words were frowned upon. They had to be linguistically fit for Empire. While there are efforts to revive Gaelic there is still less than 2% of the population who actually speak it. Despite this, Scotland continues to produce fine Gaelic poets, and three of them are represented in this anthology.

It was left to Hugh MacDiarmid to revive the use of Scots with his synthetic Lallans or Lowland Scots. He had hoped to do for Scotland what Yeats had done for Ireland. By reviving a culture that was languishing as a result of English influence, Yeats brought about a national consciousness that fed directly into radical Irish politics. This led eventually to Irish independence.

MacDiarmid sought to use Scots in exactly the same way. As Douglas Dunn put it in his introduction to the *Faber Book of Twentieth Century Scottish Poetry* in 1992—*'Scottish culture had become provincial because a nation had allowed itself to become a province.'*

While it can be said that MacDiarmid and others around him did bring about a Scottish Literary Revival, Scotland until the 1980s remained—though more culturally reinvigorated—a Labour component of Union, with Scotland regularly sending down bus-loads of Labour MPs to Westminster. It was Mrs Thatcher's conservatism with its patronising manner and personal interest before collective ones that helped foster a greater sense of national consciousness in Scotland, by Scots defining themselves as opposite to the selfish values she espoused.

Scots is in good shape today. There are many fine writers using the language. Arguably, the best two Scottish–themed poetry collections this century— William Hershaw's *The Sair Road* of 2018 and Gerda Stevenson's *Quines* of 2018 make good use of the Scots language. While Hershaw's book is almost entirely written in Scots, Stevenson's collection simply shows her versatility in both Scots and English. I am delighted that both poets have contributed poems to this anthology.

As far back as 1968 the poet George Bruce said in the book *The Scottish Literary Revival* that the strength of the Scots language *'should not be underrated.'* He went on to note *'the racy, independent, life of Glasgow and other cities'* saying there was *'a treasury there.'*

How prophetic Bruce was! Glasgow produced James Kelman and Tom Leonard, who used their Glasgow dialect to produce literary work that remains outstanding. Their choice of language was as much political as it is cultural. They speak with the voices of the people they live with. They refuse to be separated from them. Their voices demand to be heard. They demand to be heard because they have something to say and how dare anyone tell anyone else how to speak. Our speech defines who we are and how we see the world. And that world is appraised by our language and how we think through it. We are not for being demeaned by the way we talk. We are our voices. Clearly all that previous belting simply did not work.

These writers—along with others like Irvine Welsh, James Robertson, John Aberdein, Des Dillon, Jenni Fagan and Matthew Fitt—have not only revived the use of Scots but turned it into something that is vibrant in literary terms. There are a number of poets in this anthology using Scots in their poems.

Where some poets may actually be writing in English, they can also pepper their poems with Scots words which seem more apt than English words. There are some poems written in Shetlandic and Jim Mainland and Christine De Luca have kindly offered translations of some of their Shetlandic words. This all suggests a cultural confidence and awareness though Hume, of course, would be appalled.

Home

The anthology is divided into three sections—Home, Abroad and Elsewhere. All the poems have a radical edge to them and—as expected—a number deal with Scotland's constitutional debate currently taking place. Other poems in the Home section clearly have strong Scottish connotations that they could not go anywhere else.

While William Hershaw bemoans the negative reporting of Scotland yet he can still sense *'In the Eildons the adder tastes the air for change.'* And Meg Bateman in 'Iomallachd/Remoteness' suggests the Highlands are no longer remote in Scotland since we can drive there in a day. This remoteness is now to be found *'at the bleak edge of cities, in the tower-blocks between motorways where people are....edged out from power.'*

Abroad

The Abroad section shows the international dimension that many Scottish poets address. A few deal with the bizarre President across the Atlantic. Geraldine Gould writes of *'tricks from a new guy with orange hair'* while Annie McCrae puts this new guy into perspective by saying *'mendacity is on the rise.'* Magi Gibson would like to give him the treatment he gives others—*'Wrap him in tinfoil,'* she says. Chad Norman simply calls him *'a flunky.'* Jean Rafferty talks of *'blood diamond phones'* as Tom Hubbard imagines the Holy Family being given *'the hostile environment'* treatment on their arrival in the UK.

Any national demand must also be an international one to be fully acceptable. Trump, Johnson, Putin, Orban, Bolsonaro, Modi and Erdogan all reveal their risible national outlooks and that is why, without an international dimension to any politics, such outlooks will remain ugly like they all are. Jim Mainland, in his poem 'The Voices', also shows the utter shallowness of those who clearly have a stake in keeping things how they are as he writes of *'a decaying class trapped in some endless theatre of the absurd of their own making.'*

This is where Owen Gallagher and David Betteridge have the necessary antidotes. Gallagher visualises *'a new world being assembled'* where voices are *'bolted and welded into one.'* This image reminds me of the Ken Currie painting 'Template of the Future' of 1986. For this new world or a new Scotland to emerge, David Betteridge reminds us of the real elephant in the room—capitalism. All wealth is created by labour and unequal divisions accrue from it, with the capitalist receiving the lion's share. As the masses toil in every way to serve the capitalist, Betteridge gently reminds the capitalist, *'We dig your graves.'*

Elsewhere

In the section 'Elsewhere' poets deal with many of the broader social issues that concern them. Such issues, it should be said, did not spontaneously appear out of the air, they were created by the political choices made by others. A young man who goes around as *'hashtag stitches hem his cheek'* did not grow up like that, as Stephen Watt tells us in 'A Wide Berth'. He became like that through the society into which he was born. Austerity, after all, as Magi Gibson says, came *'with government-sponsored glee.'* Moreover, it came as Donald Adamson says, courtesy of *'the manipulators, the moulders of opinion.'*

Poets in this section show their concern for the plight of the homeless, in poems by Alistair Findlay, George Colkitto, Magi Gibson and Jean Rafferty, while Jim Mainland and John Tinney both take serious looks at the class divide. There are also some heartfelt poems that deal with family issues that are strained in poems by Stuart McHardy and Beth McDonough, and there are poems that show support for women by Chris Boyland, Brian Johnstone and Vivien Jones. Sheila Templeton—in the Abroad section—also raises issues affecting baby girls dumped in a refuse heap in Karachi because they are baby girls.

In one short, haunting poem by Gordon Dargie he compares *'hurcheons'* (hedgehogs) to children who have run away from care homes *'wi a coat buttoned aa the wey up'* just as a hedgehog protects itself by curling up inside. These children are then caught and returned to the *'bonfire'* of the care system. Nicloe Carter also raises this issue in 'He Spoke Lallans.'

Another aspect that poets in this section deal with is the mind control that goes hand in hand with the continued choice of inequality. Jim Ferguson rails off many of these levels of thought control as Bee Parkinson-Cameron questions should we just *'conform or die?'* Chrys Salt cleverly takes issue with the misuse of language. *'Collateral',* she says, *'is no longer money pledged against a loan'* but is now *'children burned alive in the bent wreckage of a car.'*

Nature also features in some of the poems as a vehicle for exploring certain issues. Christine De Luca watches a *'swaabie'* (a great black-backed headed gull) steal food from other birds. This bird will not go without, she says, *'nor yet his kind.'* In these few words she brings to mind Jeff Bezos, Mike Ashley, Philip Green and so many others.

Mandy Haggith writes about migrating birds as 'Immigrants' in her poem of that name. She effectively challenges the anti-immigration brigade to apply their prejudices to birds: *'In detention should fieldfares be kept apart from redwings?'* She questions if *'Perhaps they are economic migrants'*, making us consider today's human migrants. Ghazi Hussein, in addressing his adoptive city of Edinburgh, actually compares himself to *'an immigrant bird.'*

There are a number of poems that deal with war and crimes against humanity. The same forces, of course, that create poverty also create war. Lesley Benzie reminds us that many of the suspect arguments in the past are being regurgitated today and anyone wishing to know anything about the Greenham Common women should read her 'Common Rebels.'

Mary McCabe also gives the woman's angle to war as 'Stories sans Glory.' Chrys Salt, Edward Mackinnon and Hugh MacMillan feature atrocities that took place in the Middle East while Annie McCrae brings back all the horror associated with General Pinochét of Chile who was, we should remember, a friend of Mrs Thatcher.

Geordie McIntyre pleads for compassion and hope in 'New York-9-11' while it is left to Mario Relich to show how figures like 'Indiana Jones' are still shooting people of colour at will, as they once did in the Tarzan films or the *'Cowboy and Indian'* films of yesteryear. As Indiana shoots some *'tall, bearded, black-robed man'* in some *'dusty Tunisian town'* and then simply shrugs his shoulders *'smiling ironically'*, we can begin to see why it is that such black-robed men, though they can be killed, can still have *'dreams of burning skyscrapers.'*

Peter Godfrey uses chilling contrast as he eats a healthy breakfast at the Peace Camp next to the Faslane naval base that stores Trident nuclear weapons, and Geraldine Gould looks at a family photograph of former family members who will be forever missing. It is left to Kate Armstrong, in a delicately crafted poem that seeks peace, to declare: *'Each has a right to its feathers.'*

It is also a delight to see two poets who each refer to the great Gaelic poet,

Sorley Maclean. While William Hershaw sees bluebells carpeting *'Bellshill as much as in Hallaig'*, Edward Mackinnon introduces his poem 'To Sorley Maclean' with a quote from Maclean's famous poem, 'Hallaig'—*'the dead have been seen alive.'* Strangely, though for different figures, Hershaw compares Paul Robeson to Joe Hill, whereas for Mackinnon it is Sorley who has metamorphosed into a Celtic Joe Hill as he is seen internationally *'at the song-poem festivals of small nations'* with his *'white bardic hair blowing in the wind.'*

Poverty, drugs and exploitation

In 2019 the UN's Special Rapporteur, Philip Alston, told us that 14 million people live in poverty in the UK, with 4 million of those people living 50% below the poverty line. The statistics are dreadful and the Tories told him he had no clue what he was talking about. In Edinburgh, famed for its arts festivals, over 20% of the population live in poverty and have to use foodbanks. In other parts of Scotland these figures will be even higher. Behind these figures lie broken lives, alcoholism and drug addiction, violence and all kinds of exploitative abuse. 'Elsewhere' is never really somewhere else—it is much closer to home.

As Olive Ritch reads the sad notes on the bridge on Union Street, Aberdeen *'where too many sons and daughters have fallen out of troubled lives,'* A C Clarke feels for the *'young mother'* who *'queues in a draughty hall for a can of beans'* in some food-bank. And where Jean Rafferty, Magi Gibson and Alistair Findlay all see the too familiar homeless people in our streets—with Gibson describing them as *'foetal as uncurled ferns'*—George Colkitto places such social misery in context by saying that all these people are the *'casualties of a new economic order.'*

Two other statistics have to be considered. The first came with reading Peter Godfrey's poignant poem 'The Uist Boys' in which he looks back at the deaths of two lads from Uist during the First World War. Of the 157 battalions comprising the British Expeditionary Force 22 were Scottish. Of the 557,000 Scots who enlisted in all services 26.4% lost their lives. This figure compares with the loss of life in the rest of the UK standing at 11.8%.

The other set of statistics came from reading poems by Peter Mackay, Leela Soma, Henry Bell and Beth McDonough. While Peter, Leela and Henry remind us of Scotland's brutal and brutalising role in helping to secure and establish the Empire, Beth looks at 'The Insecurity of *Margaritifera Margaritifera'* in the Strathnaver area of the Highlands. By showing her concern for this freshwater mussel she recalls the treatment meted out to the Highlanders during the Clearances, when they were forced to emigrate from this area to make way for the more profitable sheep. Neglect of human needs easily turns into neglect for the environment—something D. A. Watson also deals with.

Emigration and Immigration

In *To the Ends of the Earth: Scotland's Global Diaspora* (2011) Tom Devine states that between 1825 and 1938 over 2.3 million people left Scotland for overseas destinations. A further 600,000 Scots also moved to England from 1841-1911, and during the 1920s—the high peak of emigration—some 363,000 Scots emigrated. With the ongoing democratic deficit and figures like these it seems incredible that the Union continues to survive.

While Scots went abroad, others came here and some of them are poets. Ghazi Hussein is a Palestinian poet from Syria who now lives in Edinburgh, a city he is *'proud to call...my only love.'* He came to Edinburgh, he tells us, *'stricken and aggrieved'* but in his poem 'Interesting File' he can also experience *'the ugliness of your racism'* which can clearly be both bureaucratic and personal.

Leela Soma, originally from Chennai (Madras), writes movingly of the immigrant experience of a woman she saw in her local laundrette in Glasgow. Like her, Soma once experienced the homesickness that *'rose in her like the soapy foam in the machine.'* In 'Just Things' Leela reminds us of Scotland's part in Empire where cotton, sugar cane and jute were *'just things that have made the world sweeter at the cost of human lives.'* Gerda Stevenson deals with such 'things' extremely well by looking at a sculpture and a monument in central Edinburgh, both of which have dark historical associations which she relates.

Mazigh Buzakhar, a Berber from North Africa, feels the sadness, pain and despair that brought him here. In the mountains of his former home he recalls his *'scream for liberty ... for the poor and powerless souls'.* It is to be hoped that in Mazigh's new home in Inverurie in the Grampians he can come to terms with where he has been, geographically and spiritually.

The poet Anne Connolly comes from Scotland's largest minority, Ireland. She is an accomplished writer and in 'Bee Division' she cleverly puts into perspective the carefully crafted class division that works against the interest of both the *'orange'* bees *'who are pretty'* and the *'emerald'* bees who *'are witty'* while *'the Royals and gentry...wing it on plenty.'*

The anthology is also delighted to have poems from Chrys Salt and Henry Bell. Chrys comes originally from Birmingham and she has made—and continues to make—an enormous contribution to Scottish culture. She cannot be defined by any border since she is an international writer and performer. Henry Bell, originally from Bristol, has made a considerable impact as editor of Scotland's premier literary magazine, *Gutter*. He has also written a superb —arguably the best—biography of Scotland's greatest radical and revolutionary figure, John MacLean.

One poet who is coming home in this anthology is Chad Norman from Nova Scotia. He is descended from Grants and McKinleys who left Scotland generations ago. Chad gave readings in Scotland in 2018 and it was an experience he treasures. His poem on Trump makes him more than welcome in this anthology.

Two short poems introduce the Home section and the collection more generally. One poem is called 'Lockdown' by Mandy Haggith and it is a reminder that this anthology has been produced during a time of enormous anguish due to Covid-19. This delicate haiku—as in much of Mandy's poetry —looks to nature both as a way out as she listens to *'a rustle of leaves'* while we continue *'felling ancient trees.'* While so many aspects of nature can invigorate us, we continue to destroy the source of that invigoration.

John McMahon offers an affectionate poem 'Fur the luve o ma country.' It is a deeply sincere piece of writing. His hopes for a new Scotia are perfectly legitimate ones. These hopes, however, should in no way make us hate other nations. John certainly does not. All other nations, we must always remember, are pitted against each other in pursuit of the profits for the few.

Scotland does not stand where it once did. That is in part thanks to her writers. And mention must be made of the enormous literary achievement of Alasdair Gray who wanted Scotland to live as if in the early days of a better nation. His vision was also an international one, the longer view that all radicals share, a better Scotland in a better and fairer world that is shared by all the poets in this anthology.

Acknowledgements

I would like to thank the Dundee artist Pat Donachie for putting the word out there, Aaron Bailey who kindly produced the flyer we used on the **Culture Matters** website and elsewhere, *Poets' Republic*, the Scottish Poetry Library, and Michael Byrne.

Other special words of thanks go to Mary McCabe of Scottish PEN, A C Clarke of the Federation of Writers (Scotland) and Jean Rafferty of Dove Tales. They all publicised the callout over several months and between them they helped to secure a good number of the poems in the collection.

Fiona Stewart, a Scottish artist based in Kent, has produced some stunning illustrations for *A Kist of Thistles* and a very special thanks must go to the way she has artistically interpreted some of the poems. Her beautiful images are more than illustrations to many of the poems, they add to and deepen the meanings of the poems.

Poetry can be insurrectionary according to Chrys Salt. For her *'poems all over the world are saying ENOUGH.'* Let the radical poetic insurrection begin.

Edinburgh, May 2020

HOME

discover what it means to be
radicalised by poverty

—Morag Smith from 'Inscription for the Yes House in Paisley'

Fur the Luve O Ma Country

The maist a kin offer is
ma soul
the hail ripeness
o it aw.
A peel it aff
like the skin o an orange
an wrap it aroon
Scotia.

—John McMahon

Lockdown

a rustle of leaves
story books and toilet rolls
felling ancient trees

—Mandy Haggith

Address by the Haggis

Ye knock kneed kilties
ye Saturday nicht Scotties,
ye pretend louers o poetry,
ye supper guests o misogyny
ye boutique socialists
ye lit i the wool unionists
ye Daily Mail monarchists—

ah am the fare o the poor o the airth,
Iceland tae Bangladesh,
stick the dirk in if ye dare?
Ah'll get ma ain back, here, there.
Ah am offal.

Hugh McMillan

Inscription for the Yes House in Paisley

(*after Burns Inscription for an Altar to Independence*)

You Oxbridge educated minds
who think us fools and keep your kind
in power and privilege, let go
of your dreaming spires and shrivelled souls;
discover what it means to be
radicalised by poverty
        —approach this shrine and learn from me.

Morag Smith

The Queen's Speech

So you think you own us
have taken possession

Will you feed us, water us
look after our education?

So you want to look after us?
Enslave us in your values

Have you not seen our changes
already since our devolution?

You master gifted us this—
now you want to take it away

It is as if you saw our power grow
fearing our freedom in the world

Seeing all our riches
our advancements overflowing

For Scotland is a wealthy nation
now in every single way

You do not own us
our small steps will not go back

They must keep moving forward
to complete our liberty.

Rose Ann Fraser Ritchie

The Honours of Scotland

Anchored
in unyielding granite,
where it should be.
Sculpted, painstakingly
in gold, crystal and silver,
as is fitting.
Its vibrant, mesmeric lustre
reflects a dream
of a finer Scotland,
within a better world,
where honours are shared.
And truth and transparency
reign supreme.
Oor new Holyrood
will be nane the waur o't.
Read its message.

Geordie McIntyre

Inspired by the creation of Dunblane goldsmith, Graham Stewart, which was commissioned for the new Parliament building.

The Airt o Declaration

Wabbit fae the bloody fecht, caul and weet fae weather
liggin laigh fae peel tae peel, joukin in the heather,
seekin freens in whitna airts a puckle fowk can fin them:
Flanders, France, the Hanseatics, Danes, the Hailie Feyther,
pledging tae nae earthly maister, laird, or thane or king
in fear he'll strike ye doon, or in howp tae gain likin
but tae a thocht, an abstract dream, a hauf-misshapen greenin
wintin a better nation.

Heartened fae the campaigns, caul and weet fae weather
mairchin toon tae toon, forty thoosan thegither
seekin freens in whitna airts a stateless land can fin them:
Norway, Ireland, Catalonia, Iceland, the twinty-seevin
pledging tae nae politeecians, procurers o power or labour
in fear they'll tak yer siller or in howp they'll gie ye favour
but tae a thocht, an abstract dream, a lang–established greenin
plannin a better nation.

Mary McCabe

flight

so fearsomely beautiful
and innocent and pure
he scares the proud lion
according to folklore
it may be dangerous
to unchain the unicorn
but as desire for
unfettered liberty
will at time of re-birth
be the first priority
let us unleash and bareback ride the beast
making myth reality
while breezes from infinity
refresh us to the core
we shall hurdle every boundary
healing as we soar
on a flight of the seemingly impossible
above and beyond unequal union
our hearts at last will sing of freedom
and *Alba Gu Bràth* the land of compassion

Peter Kelly

Dream States

Four more years of phony outrage
frae a wee barrel frae Skye, he says,
(an investment banker, Glasgow High)
'you'll be hearing from us,' he says,
frae 'the people of Scotland,' o aye—
is that the 45 per cent that voted Yes
minus the 36 per cent SNP voters
that voted Leave? I voted Yes
to keep Mick McGahey's federated
socialist Britain on the table, in play,
a popular democratic republic minus
Crown, Lords, and petty bourgeois
nationalists talking left and walking right.
A dream? Yes! Yes! Yes! One worth having.

Alistair Findlay

YES

Can wells,
that a long drought made bitter,
self-restore?

Can sparks,
scattered from a beaten fire,
be raked in, and fed,
and made to blaze more brightly
than before?

Can pages,
torn from a precious book,
be chased,
brought back from a high wind,
and then re-bound?

Can a city, wrecked by poverty
or war, build again, and stand again,
secure on its old ground, attaining more?

Can we, bewildernessed,
construct a narrative and a map
that leads us into wiser ways?

Can there be a spring of good
sufficient to flush clean
the flushed contaminants
that history conveys?

Can the green ribbon of a deep song,
and deep thought, extend to furthest folk
its strong tug, and bring them soon
to the dear place of peace
where we belong?

David Betteridge

Voyage of the Saltire

We are good at
tholing
dreeing
scunner and skaith
biding our time
hunkering doon
eating our livers
hanging in there
keeping a calm souch
hauding oor wheesht
we are good at
singing songs

in a wee boatie yawing
under the freight of old words
and new things
on the horizon
if not land
just keep singing
scunner and skaith
and now we know
more songs

Kate Armstrong

Whispers

Listen

Whispers—Whispers—Whispers

Hear us
Whispers—Whispers—Whispers
listening

In the darkness that may follow,
the warriors of reason will return

Hearing the call from the thunder
gasping at the changes to us all

The toxic air breathing out
lightning strikes but we regroup

Now hear the voices
eloquent and with courage

Nature whispering
even from the old oak trees

Never relenting
Never giving up

Whispers—Whispers—Whispers
from the fallen autumn leaves

There is still hope
whispering in the rain

Whispering in the mountains
lochs, the burns and wild heather

Waves crashing
whispering and listening

Whispering in the wind
reconnecting to ourselves

We are not of your making UK
our votes have all been counted

The people voted
from every single background
Scottish people living here—
we know where we belong.

Rose Ann Fraser Ritchie

It's not you, it's me

englandwalesandnorthernireland
you know but simply won't admit
this relationship, this marriage of convenience
isn't working anymore

let's not try to apportion blame
in fact I'll make it easy for you
it's not you, it's me
we want different things

we've been growing apart for some time
you must have noticed
and our differences will make us resent each other
unless we do something about it now

we need a clean break
so that we can each seek what we really want
pursue our own interests
there's no reason why we cannot remain good friends

Peter Kelly

Paul Robeson at Woolmet Colliery, 1949

Then rauchle tongues fell lown,
piece crusts were puit doun,
snap tins sneckit
and big men looked wee.

The Coal Giant hisel,
glisteran muckle-man,
genie o the tyauvit seam,
kittlin his anthracite banes,
had sclimmed up the dreepan pit
tae croun tae us in the canteen.

Singan in a vyce mair true
than steel pick dirlan on lunkhart stane,
kythin clearer than a pirl o fresh watter,
trummelin wi mair howp than a braith o clean air.

Our coal stour brous anointed,
his sang sained us then and there.
I dreamed I saw Paul Robeson last nicht,
alive as you and me.

William Hershaw

Mauchle—rough, lown—still, tyauvit—twisted, kittlin—making ready, lunkhart—large roof stone, kythin—rising, trummelin—trembling, sained—blessed

Alma Mater

Only the footprint
of the place that made me what I'm not
is still there behind the barbed wire
and buddleia, dandelion clocks
rise in the air as they did then;
we blew away the hours, counted down
to the day this wouldn't matter

We girls of slender hopes
one whose blonde hair shed feathers
from her father's budgerigars, one
who slammed doors, kept her secrets close,
silenced proposals and kind enquiries,
with a stony blink, one whose Ouija board
revealed the future

All share the same tattoos,
scratched on skin, the whirr of sewing machines,
boys talking only football, smell of
chlorinated water,
the need to leave and yet belong, free
dinners, the older brother already gone,
the knack of choosing

No grand reunion
on Carbeth and Sunnylaw; wings
of cabbage white and painted ladies throng
in a meadow; the hymn of the old school
was never written down, its howls and grace notes
lie quiet in the brick dust now—still
our steps are singing

Morag Smith

Henry Dundas, 1st Viscount Melville

Born and died in Edinburgh, 1742-1811, the most influential politician in the British Government of his time: Home Secretary, War Secretary, Chief Secretary for India, and First Lord of the Admiralty.

You may bleat your outrage,
but it's beneath me, and won't take its toll.
I'm above all that, solid as my column,
and mighty as the Empire I strove to build—
I'm a Scot, after all, and can thole time's weather.
Granted, we lost America under my watch,
but my sights were always high enough
to view the long game. Tell me this:
did your forebears complain
when my single-word amendment to the Bill
prolonged the slave trade's gravy train?
They were content, I think, to sup with me
the profits for another generation.
I got things done—reined Ireland in,
took India, rolled out the penal colony
in Botany Bay, corralled South Africa,
my favourite child, into the fold:
Hear the ring of a global brand:
Melville, Dundas from land to land!
The winds of change might blow me down,
but I've earned the heft of every block
you've built to laud me on this plinth.

Gerda Stevenson

NOTE: Dundas supported Wilberforce's Bill in Westminster to abolish slave trading but added the word 'gradually' as an amendment, which anaesthetised the Bill, allowing the capturing and trading of another half million slaves for at least a further 15 years.

James Keir Hardie

Tae Friedrich Engels ye were the *super cunning Scot ... with demagogic tricks*
—and he wisnae sookin in. Hud he been a kirkie mannie,
he'd huv been doon oan his knees, pittin up a wird
makin siccar ye niver got nar sniffin distance o Westminster.
His girnin wraxed new heichts faan ye waaked throu that door,
claith bunnet an homespun, spleet-new Member for West Ham.

Nae fur you the cauld analysis, the lang-nebbit theory o the dialectic
settin the warld tae richts, Aa yer gumption, yer scrievin, yer wirds
cam fae life, fae a day's lang darg, fae the hard tyauve o yer hauns
burnt intae muscle memory—aa these oors sittin in the derkness
ten year auld, listenin for the rummle o each loaded cairt
managing tae practise yer letters gin ye'd a caunle stump.

Men voted for ye ower the heids o the weel-gaithert, the swall-heidit,
the high- bendit. An it wisnae jist cause o yer kittlin-up wirds,
though you cud start a bleeze in ony owdience—aye, an relish it!
Workin fowk were gizzent in weys the theorists hud nae idea.
But you did—an mair. Ilka chiel that voted for ye kent yer years in the pit,
pyochered the coal blaik in yer lungs, daured the beat o yer contermit hert.

Nae that ye were athoot principle. Ye were niver a pragmatist. An wirds
were yer freens. A scriever in papers, leaflets, aftentimes awa fae hame
warld traiveller, warly wise—yet ye keepit yer watch at Cumnock time

for I could tell then, what was going on at home...
when the children went to school, when they returned
when they went to bed...

For that alane, I'd huv voted fur ye.

Sheila Templeton

The State of the Nation

Two hundred years being wrapped snug in tartan
made to sing 'God Save the Queen'
your forefathers say,' Be a proud son of Scotland'
but in this day and age what do they mean?
We're all rebels and princes, fighters and lovers
feeling on top of the world
oh the few who will feature on the pages of school-books
and the many who'll never be heard

We're solving the mystery without any proof
oh enough of your lies, won't you tell me the truth?
Are we up to our necks in the blood of Jock Tamson's bairns?
All the sugar, tobacco, cotton, molasses
looking at history through rose-tinted glasses
nemo me impune lacessit, and other such joys

Be you Scottish or British or English or Irish
tick the box for your colour or creed
cultural appropriation on a packet of biscuits is the only real reference I need
from Ossian's diaries to the Highland Societies
inclusion behind padlocked doors
but the word 'Caledonian' was coined by the Romans
just to mark out the mad bastards up north

Is it 'yes' is it 'no', is it getting beaten 3-0 at home?
Is it a pregnant teenager at the end of a phone?
But she hasn't the time to read *Rob Roy* nor *Ivanhoe*
nothing to do so go out for a pint, eh?
The blue-blooded bowler hats shout '1690'
next generation take heed and sharpen their swords

All suited and booted, all dressed up to the nines
in a Royal Stewart kilt from some factory line
'Made in China' hiding away under a plastic cockade

Is it brains over brawn? Is it link over lorne?
Is it choosing the right football team?
The echoed frustrations in a half-empty Hampden
with Gemmill, Dalgleish and Gordon McQueen
how do you feel about God or the Deil?
The 'Flowers of the Forest' for sale?
The young ones who pay for their parents' transgressions
while the old ones rehash the old tales

Night by 15.30, cold mince and tatties
a wink to the lads and a toast to the lassies
a night at *'Her Majesty's Pleasure'* to round it all off
the blue and the white on a sky of slate grey
the grovelling politicos with nothing to say
but it's hard getting by given neither the time nor the day

Hey for *'Bobbin John'*, hey for cockolorum
Tha tighin fodham, fodham, fodham
oh well you take the high road and I'll take the low
the *'Skyscraper Wean's'* got nowhere to go
now the blue paint's all smudged on the face
of the star of the show

Louis Rive

Not Nuart Aberdeen

Note after handwritten note
reaches out in the breeze of passers-by,
stopping them on the bridge on Union Street
where too many sons and daughters have fallen
out of troubled lives. Looking down at rail tracks,

I mutter their names. On this warm spring day
between Good Friday and Easter Sunday, I mingle
with shadows on the bridge, reading stories, brave
and desperate, of those struggling with dark days.
A grieving mother says, *something must be done.*

Taking down every note attached to bridge railings
is not the answer, dear councillors of Aberdeen,
nor is a higher barrier. As one note reads,
the lack of services is the problem,
not the height of the bridge.

Dear councillors, listen
and extend a hand to help
                                        everyone
cross the bridge on Union Street.

Olive M Ritch

Mary, Queen of Scots

This week I watched a film that suggested
Darnley was gay and took for a lover
Rizzio, Mary's secretary, also
Scotland was a place of beautiful hills,
desolate castles, forlorn beaches and
very few people, apart from those
in John Knox's church but even they
were averse to going outside and
rioting or just going about their
days. I could see that this film was trying
to show Mary in all her dimensions
yet failed, reminding me of everything
written about her because—who wrote it?
Mary was Queen in a deck stacked so high
against her that no tale untouched by that
could be told. Kenny says in bad places
it's still like that and I say to judge one
place as bad requires looking around.
Have we come so far? Have our tale tellers
moved beyond comparing the shapeliness
of our leaders' calves? In his youth, Henry,
Mary's uncle, had very fine ankles.

Cara L. McKee

Billy Fullerton

In response to Edwin Morgan's 'King Billy'

Razor gang founder, Mosley Blackshirt,
He's where he should be—in the dirt.
Let the gently cerebral
Feast on this waster's funeral:
I won't sell myself for a song.
And, yes, it will be—for as long
As we lend credence to such stuff—
Grey over Riddrie right enough.

David Cameron

We Were Being Good
Or a Wanker came on at Merkland Street

So I get on a train full of Rangers fans,
and I'm reading a book on the Easter Rising,
and I'm feeling a bit self-conscious.

Then these six Celtic lads get on at Govan. Steaming.
Can of Dragon Soop each.
Everyone's shouting,
the driver comes back to see what the trouble is,

but everyone says they're having fun and no-one wants any bother.
And the driver's like, 'keep it that way lads.'
But of course, the second the train sets off, everyone's up on their feet
singing, and banging the walls of the train:

'Zombies,' 'Big Jock knew.'
You know the score.

And I'm sitting there trying to read,
learning about branches of the Irish Brotherhood in pre-World War One Glasgow.
And thinking about how football is the worst.

Then, as we're pulling into Partick,
this old boy, covered in union jacks, walks the length of the carriage.
All the way up to the Bhoys end.
And he stands there,
blocking them in,
chest puffed out
and he says:

'Fair play to ye lads, sjist a game an we're aw the same underneath, aye.'

And then he shakes each one of their hands.

And at that moment, as we're stopped at Partick
and this old man is patting one of the young Celtic lads on the back,
right then,
a guy in a Rangers scarf steps on to the train and spits
square in the face of a boy in a green track-suit.

The man in the scarf jumps off the train,
the train doors shut,
and the boy wipes the yellow spit that's dripping down his face and says:

'But we were being good.'

Henry Bell

Fill, Fill a Rún Ó

We all sang Fill, Fill a Rún Ó. A tremble on the lip of piety.
Such a rendering of sorrow for that mother pleading
with her son, a priest, to find the hard road home.
We knew he'd chosen change from Catholic ways
to Protestant simplicity. My grandmother's path.

And that's where the real sorrow lies, born from suspicion
seen in the eyes of centuries. Myopic distain
and hatred in the festered burden of the years.
A harrowing of heads and hearts.

The politics of faith were never more pernicious. Yet look
at where we've reached on blitzed bones, a frozen shoulder
of presumption. Our parish priest has stepped across
from Anglican. A married man with sons who's fled
the very thought of female bishops. Such ambiguity!

What would we have done if petrified on Easter afternoon
we'd scurried off afraid of consequences, seen the scourge
of sanctity gone too far and God alone knowing what
might come? Would we have spat a frozen judgment
at the man who joined us on the getaway road, silenced
the stranger who sought to reach us all?

Anne Connolly

Fill a Rún Ó (Gaelige) means *Come back my darling.*

Wan wirld at Bluemull Soond

Linga bracks da Bluemull Soond,   *the Isle of Linga breaks*
smooth as a neesick.   *porpoise*
Tirricks lift fae ferry furrows,   *arctic terns*
sweep backwards in circles,
skoitin fur sillocks: dey dive   *peering purposefully for young saithe*
an rise in perfect verticals.
Anidder ferry comes an still dey laav: *hover*
whit strug fur sic a peerie paek.   *struggle, tiny morsel*

Alang da banks   *cliffs*
a swaabie tips an penks,   *great black-headed gull walks jauntily*
traepin fur maet.   *nagging for food*
Tief at he is, he shastes dem   *thief, chases them*
till dey drap der catch.

He'll no fant,   *not go famished*
nor yet his kind,
while peerie tirricks fish
da Bluemull Soond.

Christine De Luca

47

The Insecurity of *Margaritifera Margaritifera*

Precious few mussels still cling to old places,
after hardened factors in the Naver's dark life.
Already, too many have been wrested from beds.

Our deeply-nacred pearls' wild space is fragile.
Note habitats, completely lost from Ythan,
borders and beyond. Surviving—just—in Sutherland.

No-one can reverse that lasting anxiety,
when we recognise great damage done.
Too many stones are loose; others, overturned.

There are returns, but not enough to reassure
the vulnerable they will be cherished;
not simply prised off, but sustained.

Plenty wealthy men stand thigh-deep,
wading in the thick of it, ready to chart
salmon's migratory patterns, pay in cash.

Ghost–still boats go nowhere on the loch.
The licensed flirt their flies, catch what they like,
untroubled by what's stolen from the Naver.

Beth McDonough

Note: Some of the most painful scenes of the Scottish Clearances occurred in Strathnaver.

Orwell in Jura

Orwell liked to be solitary,
like Crusoe lost in his island.

Leaving his sister and adopted son
at his landlord's cottage in Jura,

nothing gave him more pleasure
than to do a spot of exploration.

In his Diary he noted hoodie crows,
and the soil dry as a bone, quite stony.

Not very far away he could see,
the sea desolate, yet invigorating,

a seal slowly rising and sinking down,
its nose perpendicular like a porpoise.

An eagle some way off, he wondered
if it was really some kind of buzzard.

Two young cuckoos he saw sitting on a fence,
and (he wasn't too sure) a gold-crested wren.

At times it was very hot, dry and still all day,
the sea like glass, and then five minutes of rain.

Once he walked to Glengarrisdale, and found
an old human skull, lying on the beach there,

possibly all that remained from a massacre
of the MacLeans by the Campbells.

The skull, he surmised, was probably
not less than two hundred years old.

Next day, he observed tits with a nest
in the iron gatepost, seeing them

coming out of the hole occasionally.
One got momentarily stuck in the hole,

just as he approached them to be of help,
only to find that it shrieked in terror.

Orwell wrote *Nineteen Eighty-Four*
in his exile from devastated London,

but he had 1947 really on his mind,
suspecting every casual visitor

might be Stalin's secret agent. He listened
to the wireless grimly every morning

crackling with news of jackboots stamping
on faces in Poland, Palestine, and Greece.

Mario Relich

To Edinburgh

City of towers and turrets
city of my desire
I sought you as an immigrant bird
full of yearning and a song on my lips
beautiful city of hills
adornment of Earth
a particular paradise
I came to you stricken and aggrieved
restore me with your fragrance
my heart's song will find its rhythm
in your branches I build my nest
and there I was reborn
although long before I knew you, I declared my love
city of purity, in you I am at home
your people are my people
by covenant of faith
how can I ever repay you?
no word or poem
would be enough
I want to say
I am proud to call you my only love
I beg your forgiveness if I impose on you
but there is always a martyr in the question of love
one must be the lover, the other the loved.

Ghazi Hussein

Hurcheons

Nuthin came oot aboot the hame fir years
except fir the weans that kept runnin awey
wi naewhere tae run tae. Then we pit them back.

Ye kent ye were in fir a quiet run,
a wean wi a coat buttoned aa the wey up
an nuthin tae say in the back o the car.

Yir telt tae check fir hurcheons in a bonfire.
Av picked them up an pit them on the flames
an tried a joke tae bring them oot a bit.

Gordon Dargie

Hurcheons — hedgehogs

The Uist Boys

In the bitter wind of Ypres
two mates seek repose:
young MacPherson in his greatcoat,
slung rifle etched with snow

and, hands thrust deep in worsted,
on an icy wooden bench
Ewen Nicholson from Grimsay,
front line in the firing trench,

with his thin knees and glengarry hat,
wispy trace of tash and beard,
lips drawn tight, short of a smile,
as if seeing the end he fears.

They are cornered by their duty,
brass and khaki uniform,
made to gun down the marauding Boche.
Ewen sends a snapshot home

six days before his slaughter.
Now they share a Flanders grave—
lads who'd never live to savour
the press of an embrace.

Peter Godfrey

Iomallachd

Chan eil iomallachd sa Ghàidhealtachd ann—
le càr cumhachdach
ruigear an t-àite taobh a-staigh latha;
's e luimead na h-oirthir
a shàraich na doine
is a chuir thar lear iad
a tha gar tàladh an-diugh,
na làraichean suarach a dh'fhàg iad
cho miannaichte ri gin san rìoghachd.

Och, an iomallachd, càit a bheil thu?
Càit ach air oir iom nam bailtean,
sna towerblocks eadar motorways
far am fuadaichear na doine
gu iomall a' chumhachd,
an aon fhiaradh goirt nan súilean
's a chithear an aodann sepia nan eilthireach
(a bha mise riamh an dùil
gum biodh an Nàdar air dèanamh àlainn).

Remoteness

The Highlands are not remote any more—
with a powerful car
you can reach the place in a day;
it is the bleakness of the coast
that wore the people down
and sent them overseas
that draws us today,
the miserable sites they left
as desired as any in the land.

Alas, remoteness, where are you?
Where, but at the bleak edge of the cities,
in the towerblocks between motorways
where people are removed,
edged out from power,
the same hurt squint in their eyes
as is seen in the emigrants' sepia faces
(I had fully expected
Nature to have made beautiful).

Meg Bateman

Dìomhanas

Nach sibh a tha moiteil
às na h-oidhirpean agaibh
fraoich fhàs ann an talamh aoil;
le mòr shaothair
agus mòr mhaoineachaidh
thig sìthean air, gun teagamh.

Ach, na toiribh a-mach
às na taighean-glainne e
no seargaidh e
sa bhad

'S fhad's a tha sibh ris an obair seo
tha fraoich na mòintich
a' fannachadh
le dith uisge
's na gàirnealairean uile
anns na taighean-gloinne
à strì ri lusan
air nach fàs freumh.

Futility

Aren't you proud
of your efforts
to grow heather in clay soil;
with much work
and much funding
it will bloom, certainly.

But don't take it out
of the greenhouses
or it will wither
instantly.

And while you're thus occupied
the heather on the moor
wilts
for lack of water
while all the gardeners
are in the greenhouses
looking after plants
on which no roots will grow.

Anne c Frater/ Anna c Frater

He Spoke Lallans

Words didn't, don't, come cheap
weren't always everyone's right
words can soothe a tortured soul
or start a war

Words are gold, diamonds, platinum
priceless
to me

The spoken word
a conversation
can make my body tingle
my heart flutter with joy
like manna feeding my spirit
or it can fill my day, my week
with gloom

I've heard it said,
'The world would be a better place
if we used less words
and made more positive actions,'
the words of an Animal Behavioural
Psychologist, no less

While I believe this may be true
to WANT to use positive, kind words
is not necessarily what everyone
feels like doing

The ability to read and write is often
taken for granted
I knew a man who, at the age of 21
couldn't do either

he spoke Lallans
not *proper* English

Different demographics
different circumstances
he could have been a brain surgeon
but
he was homeless
he was just another cog
in the mechanism of the facilitated
vicious cycle of Care Home abuse
homelessness and prostitution
well- what were his options?
what were mine when I was homeless?
I can read, write and speak English fluently
I was indoctrinated to do so
Words can give hope or
take it away
words can bring people together
or push them apart
words can heal
words can get you a roof over your head
employment
and food to eat
or strip you of these basic needs

If someone who has a so called *'rough accent'*
said exactly the same phrase
as someone who has a
so called *'well-spoken accent'*
who would you respect more
which one would seem more employable?
which one would you trust?

Please don't judge people by how they speak
their accent
or use of vocabulary
please never let our traditional
Scottish languages disappear

Nicole Carter

The Sacred Breakfast

Muesli, blueberries, soya milk
five yards from the road
and traffic pounding.

Lacework of sun, woodsmoke,
an insect on the page,
the morning waking.

Raspberries in the hedgerow,
an oystercatcher's squeal,
razor wire billowing

mile upon mile,
cartwheel of knives.
Warheads slip beneath the sea.

A driver hoots,
our sooted kettle,
easy steps on the muddy path.

Peter Godfrey, Faslane Peace Camp, 2017

Unlawful

The inquest found and ruled
      that the 19-year-old man from POLLOK,

who had attended BONNYHOLM primary school,
who had been lawfully unemployed,
who was persuaded of the benefits of a military career
by the army recruitment officers at his local job centre
and who had been kissed goodbye at GLASGOW CENTRAL by his lawful mother,
(who knew she wouldn't see him again)
and was killed in BASRA less than a month after he went to IRAQ
by an I.E.D. (improvised explosive device),
shrapnel severing the artery that supplies blood
to the brain, while in a store-room
only 900 metres away was a bomb-jamming device
that should have been fitted to his vehicle
(an armoured LAND ROVER on which he had volunteered
to be a top-cover sentry) had it not been for a clerical error
by the MINISTRY OF DEFENCE,

was unlawfully killed.

Edward Mackinnon

Reporting Scotland

Relentless the roadkill
counted on your crooked road,
you hang their carcasses on our screens.
Endless your litany of negatives.
In Scotland today only:
murder, rape, accident, death,
failure, allegation and sleekit attack.
So what that in Stornoway a bairn laughed on a swing,
a man in Perth let his neighbour win at Dominoes.
A woman from Methil escaped from Hell
graduating with first class honours?
You presume to edit our day,
let nothing good be heard,
as if you laundered out the clean
leaving only stains.

But a rumour has got out,
circulates the land like a breeze.
In the Eildons the adder tastes the air for change,
the hawk on Mull hangs still and listening,
bluebells carpet the wood of birches
in Bellshill as much as in Hallaig.
The old wolf has been seen in the forest.

William Hershaw

ABROAD

Just as great John MacLean of your clan parades
through other broken streets, loved and despised,
holding untouchable hands in Bihar.

—Edward Mackinnon from 'To Sorley MacLean'

Do not think that they who love their own country must hate and despise
other nations, or wish for war, which is the remnant of barbarism.

—Socialist Commandment 9 from *Socialist Sunday Schools*

I see how folk live that hae riches;
But surely poor-folk maun be wretches!

—Robert Burns, 'The Twa Dogs'

The Insurrection of Poetry

Poems are on the march.
They are singing
from the rubble of Ground Zero,
the ruins of Damascus and Sarajevo,
the bomb shelters of Amiriyah,
the poisoned bodies of Halabja,
from the mouths of murdered men folk
in Srebrenica.

Poems are growing from their winding sheets
in the mud and trenches
of butchered nature.
Their guns fire white poppies.
Their flags are the colour of rainbow.
Their hands fold paper cranes
under the olive trees.
From the bones of mutilated generations
they grow blossoms of resurrection.

Listen
you tyrants, murderers,
fundamentalists, mutilators,
rapists, occupiers,
racists, persecutors,
autocrats, crucifiers,
fanatics, torturers, liars,
obfuscators, manipulators,
warmongers,

silencers,

Listen!

Poems all over the world
are saying

ENOUGH.

Chrys Salt

A Pantoum of Prime Time for Liars, Mistruths and Pants on Fire

Can you spot a liar in the age of lies?
Will he scratch his head, will she shift her eyes?
When idle chatter flits with post-truth flies,
they hover on our screens in slick disguise.

Will he scratch his head, will she shift her eyes,
dealing out the word in neatly spun replies?
They hover on our screens in slick disguise,
White House to workplace, they're everywhere these guys.

Dealing out the word in neatly spun replies,
clever tweets, repeated tropes, all appear so wise,
White House to workplace, they're everywhere these guys.
Honesty has had its day, mendacity is on the rise.

Clever tweets, repeated tropes, all appear so wise.
When idle chatter flits with post-truth flies
honesty has had its day, mendacity is on the rise.
Can you spot a liar in the age of lies?

Annie McCrae

little white lies

of course I love you, always did
no priest or nun ever touched a kid
lewinsky's dress was stained with glue
hitler's diaries—every word was true
benito's trains were never late
at hillsboro' they forced the gate
brexit promises on a bus
your nhs is safe with us
bill clinton never did inhale
your arse is not sized like a whale
diseased potatoes starved a nation
einstein failed examinations
wmd found in iraq
margaret thatcher had our backs

each truth above no cause for libel
i'd swear that on a king james bible

Colin Rutherford

The Smirkin Rich

there's no yet been
a God inventit
wha said the rich
maun own the laun;
there's no beena bible wrote
that said the puir maun
scraitch fer feedin;

yet there's plenty
haver on
o god, o grace
an justice
an shak their bibles
like battleaxes at the puir
wha's scraitchin feeds them
while
the rich
look on
an
smirk.

Stuart McHardy

The Museum of Memory

The Museum of Memory
in Chatila
is little more than a shack
that reeks of oil
and cigarette smoke.
It holds old pots and pans,
faded papers, documents,
other tat.

There are no videos,
or interactive panels.
No curator
much of the time,
but people wander in
and out to smell
or touch or sit
in the mess of the past.

History is not much
more than a joke,
the ghosts
of men and maps,
but memories
are something else,
especially the memories
that are not our own.

Kamel holds
his grandfather's key,
huge, made from solid iron,
the key to a locked door
of a locked house
a farm left in haste

a blur of years ago
and all these things

are dust now,
the walls gone,
the furniture broken,
the trees torn down
all lost beyond the key only,
which Kamel turns
over and over in his palm
and unlocks air.

Hugh McMillan

The Borders

The borders
lie deep in maroon Jamaica,
Freetown,
and Jericho.
Men made from tar ten thousand years ago
who walked for generations north
go home and pillage, rob
and leave a hundred pipe bands in return.
Bodies that trudged from Africa to Orkney
return white and cold and thieving.
They leave Nubians their tartan trews
and whisky
and take bodies, gold and food
and law.
The Scottish Borders stretch
across the central belt and up
through Aberdeen, a great gulf
filled with wealth and pride and torn black skin
hiding words like merchant, sugar,
Lord, tobacco, lookout.
Look out.

Henry Bell

Just Things

Cotton, soft to the skin, the perfect bedlinen
or starched heavy, flattened with coal-heated iron,
bleached, dyed in different shades, batik designed,
years of slavery running through strung out veins.

Sugar, cane rich, green and tall under the tropical sun,
nurtured, tended and cultivated to sweeten our tongues,
crushed and juice extracted, pure molasses, thick and brown
like the bodies of those auctioned welts marked like lines of cane.

Jute, the humble vegetable fibre, soft and shiny grown in East Bengal,
made into coarse, hessian, gunny bags to hold rice and twisted into rope.
A billion jute sandbags despatched from the British Empire in India
to the trenches in World War I for those who died in that futile war.

Bales of cotton streaked and branded with the blood of slaves,
bags of jute imprinted and inscribed with colonial stamps,
fields of cane sugar made into molasses and golden syrup—
just things which have made the world sweeter
at the cost of human lives.

Leela Soma

The Contamination of Red

When the crowd is gathered
and I happen to be on the hill
it is then I can see all of
what the Smart TV has captured,
what I must say to myself
is a crowd gathered for worship
strangely made up of ties and ball-caps
all of them for worship,
a choice to begin the chant
loud in my mind instead of sleep
preventing me from feeling well
as the chant quickly becomes
the alarm-clock I never set,
a type of annoyance or disturbance
both dangerous and irresistible,
a chant going on and on like this:

Trump is not a turd wearing a tie!
Again:
Trump is not a turd wearing a tie!

A tie each time the crowd moves
I can see is red, yes, a red tie,
hanging from a neck, not hanging
the neck I often saw hanging him
in a dream, the *him* being known
by other than my dream, known
to be as red as the neck it
was around, or was it a *him*
who also sported a red ball-cap
with certain letters on the front,
letters I believe to be a lie
intentional, sewn into that cap

to eventually reveal his need
to mislead, to ultimately be
what exposes him to be an
imposter, a flunky attempting
to play the role of president.

The contamination of red, yes,
the colour red, is taking me over,
I can no longer tolerate a tie.
I can no longer wear or watch
a red ball-cap, but the crowd
made up of voters ready to
see their hatred illuminated
across the necks and foreheads,
a generation eager to forget
the peoples they put in boats
now heading for any port
Canada will wait at, waving
a flag offering a loving white
and a red still uninfected and free.

Chad Norman

The President Visits for a Quick Round

And when he lands, demand the laces
from his shoes. Make him descend

the steps of Air Force One, brogues
flip-flopping, watch as he shuffles

in the effort not to trip. On the tarmac whip
the belt from his golfing trews, try not

to smile as he clasps them as they slip,
check through his papers at the passport gate,

flick the pages, stroke your chin and frown,
suck air in noisily through pursed lips, tap

on your computer screen, silently stride off, return,
scrutinize him head to toe as if the very sight

would make you spew, strip him of his dignity,
crumple and toss it in a bin just beyond

his reach, then separate him from
his startled wife, bundle him along

a corridor, lights flickering, push him through
an armour-plated door marked ALIEN.

Incarcerate him in a cage. Wrap him in tinfoil.
Tell him to wait; his case has been referred

for further, full investigation. No discussion
can be entered into. Due process will be followed.

And no! No reasons need be given. He
is our guest now. Oh, and—*fáilte!*

Did we say *fáilte*? Welcome.

Magi Gibson

Atlantic

Some giant had the name first,
hailed from Greece, down Santorini way,
was tricked into holding up the sky, they say,
by an even bigger-muscled guy. Fearless,
they clashed for just a bunch of apples.

Books took on the name, mountainous worlds
mapped out beyond the pillars, before
a river so vast it encompassed everything,
separating east from west.
Did someone guess what was to come?

Ah, new world, old world,
now we get it. The river has poured
into a pond, the boats are clanking
with remembered chains. No more
heroes across this ocean, just tinkling
tones, and crazy talk of walls and fencing,
tricks from a new guy with orange hair.
He is standing on waves of fear. Dappled
fruits swell, preparing to fall, or burst.

Geraldine Gould

21st Century Blues
(inspired by Deryn Rees-Jones' 'Liverpool Blues')

The high towers burning fiercely, the sea awash with boats,
armed guards at border checkpoints, bombs triggered by remotes.
Thick smoke is rising, spreading from a hundred hecatombs.

In Syria, in Kabul, in Mosul, in Palestine
though stars dance in the evening sky, and sun won't cease to shine
the earth is heaped with those whose sleep is colder than their tombs.

To New York, Paris, Manchester, to London and Marseilles
the terrorist comes armed with faith to blow all doubts away
while muddled men tweet fear and hate from dark and lonely rooms.

The streets are rough with sleepers, estates are tough with knives
bundles in West End doorways are begging for their lives
young hearts break in the crossfire of a gangraped afternoon.

We sleepwalk through this chaos the way we've always done.
Though every muscle tells us that it's time to cut and run:
the roads are blocked, the gates are locked, a curfew twilight looms.

The ballot box divides and rules, the voters are fed lies
the ether swarms with hashtag posts buzzing like angry flies.
We want the tempo different but are slow to change the tune.

We want the clutter swept away but shy at the new broom.
We want the tempo different but don't dare to change the tune.

A C Clarke

New York, 9-11

In slow motion instant
beating hearts are stilled
with sabre scythe-certainty.
A bitter harvest is reaped,
canyons of life reduced
to cairns of desolation.
Echoes to infinities,
maelstroms of malice
swirl in an inferno of dust
settling in a wasted land
where seeds of love, compassion, hope
must be sown...

Geordie McIntyre

Written 25/9/01

Remembrance Day

The top brass in immaculately tailored
military frock coats, their buttons and boots
polished within an inch of their privileged lives,
to reflect their solemnity
for those who died in previous wars.

This unquestioning silence
is a hundred years since the first
to commemorate the end of World War I
in which seventeen million people died
in: *the war to end all wars.*

The top brass are flanked
by the last of the World War II veterans.

Their heads held high, their bodies frail
and sickle-shaped with the weight
of bravery pinned to their chests
and the memories of comrades
whose bodies and minds were broken
amid the relentless din
of staccato gunfire and aerial bombing

and even when not under fire
the sound of the mud and blood mix
as they moved around in trenches,
sucking at their souls
and rotting skin from bone
so that it clung to the insides
of fragmented boot leather
and dreams bound forever
with the sounds of death
from the boys, become men, become

boys again, whimpering their last
for their mothers.

Who also died in their droves amongst
around eighty million civilian and military deaths.

In this two minutes' silence,
are they remembering just those they knew
or reflecting on any of the many lessons
from history?

Hitler's devious and previous criminal form
was never an impediment to his rise to power
on the basis of approach that stated:

All propaganda has to be popular
and has to accommodate itself
to the comprehension of the least intelligent
of those whom it seeks to reach.

As such, he was hailed a saviour
from the austerity that dogged most ordinary
Germans' lives. While their economy collapsed
amid government mismanagement
of their balance of payments for both war
and peace.

He is not the last but possibly the first master
to twist the truth and the will of the people

willing to follow

till only the facades of bombed-out buildings
stood, their hollowed windows
like the souls of the defeated Germans

made to file past the vast piles of Jewish bodies
starved and gassed
for the world of ills
that lives inside the hearts
of the instigators and perpetrators.

As Hitler's imitators trawl our social media
and drop pop-ups instead of flyers from the ether,
sycophants to right-wing leaders
draw attention away from their political crimes.

Instead migrants and Europe are cast as the enemy
as the Daily Mail chimes in unison
congratulating itself
for its patriotism and solemn remembrance
of those who made the ultimate sacrifice.

While commenting on which designer dress
the Duchess of Sussex is wearing.

It's almost possible to hear the bleating of
'we won the war and beat the Nazis,'
as touching photographs and grainy newsreel
footage of the Kindertransports
are paraded in the tabloids and on mainstream TV.

As if edited out and left on the cutting-room floor,
there's no sign of their Jewish parents and over half-a-million
Jewish asylum-seekers who were excluded from Britain
and left behind in Nazi Europe.

Then, as now, the *Daily Mail*'s headline of 1938
berates the victims: *The way stateless Jews
from Germany are pouring in from every port
of this country is becoming an outrage...*

as it buffs the nationalistic jackboots grinding
their heels on the bloodied carcass of truth
and it's swept from our collective memory
that Hitler's war floundered in Russia.

While we're encouraged to pride ourselves
for being plucky Brits
and separate ourselves from the longest period
of peace and stability in European history.

The disenfranchised rant about the will of the people
and vote for politicians eager to carve out a society
that will see us hang forever
on the coat-tails of an 'ally'
who is armed to the teeth,
always gritted and bared to thwart any defiance,
always prepared to send many more youngsters
from the homes of the poverty-stricken
than from those of the rich,
over the top again
whenever, wherever.

Lesley Benzie

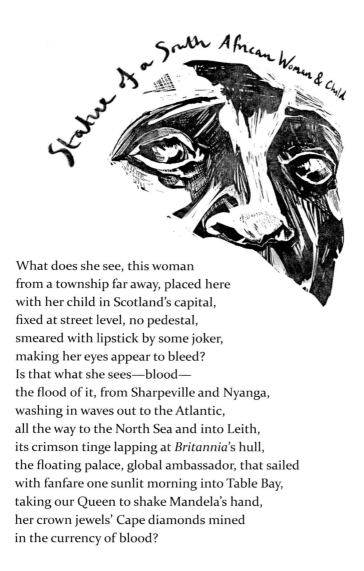

Statue of a South African Woman & Child

What does she see, this woman
from a township far away, placed here
with her child in Scotland's capital,
fixed at street level, no pedestal,
smeared with lipstick by some joker,
making her eyes appear to bleed?
Is that what she sees—blood—
the flood of it, from Sharpeville and Nyanga,
washing in waves out to the Atlantic,
all the way to the North Sea and into Leith,
its crimson tinge lapping at *Britannia*'s hull,
the floating palace, global ambassador, that sailed
with fanfare one sunlit morning into Table Bay,
taking our Queen to shake Mandela's hand,
her crown jewels' Cape diamonds mined
in the currency of blood?

Gerda Stevenson

*The sculpture 'Woman and Child' by Anne Davidson is in Festival Square,
Edinburgh. It was commissioned by the City Council to honour all those
killed or imprisoned in South Africa for their stand against apartheid,
unveiled in 1986.*

Indiana Jones

Your quest was to find the Raiders of the Lost Ark,
Nazi fanatics, searching for them in the souks
and alleyways of a dusty Tunisian town, its crowds
of Arabs looking for bargains, or eager to give you
a sales pitch. You'd already bought a pet monkey
holding on to your shoulder, screeching at anyone
so bold as to get too near his master in a white hat.

While you shield the sun from your eyes, a tall,
bearded, black-robed man rushes out of nowhere
and waves his scimitar at you, his taunting snarl
a real threat. You just shrug your shoulders,
smiling ironically, suave in your self-regard,
and take out a revolver always well-hidden,
but ready to use at any time, like right now.

One shot is all it takes, and your attacker crumbles
before you, his life snuffed out, but not his dreams
of burning skyscrapers. All the others scatter quickly,
or stand in sullen silence. You said about the Nazis
you're hunting: 'I hate those guys!' If these killers
play dirty, *might is right* their creed, take a look
in the mirror: hand on heart, how different are you?

Mario Relich

Whoso list to hunt

Sibhs' a tha dèidheil air an t-seilg
no bhith glacadh na gaoithe le ur lìon,
's eòl dhomh far a bheil eilid

air nach fhaigh sibh cothrom na Fèinne.
Oirre ann am faclan de dhaoimeann:
I'm Caesar's. Don't touch.

Ach ge b' oil leis an toirmeasg,
saltair gu h-aotrom sa chiaradh
lùb agus fuasgail an ròp

agus bheir am fiadh air falbh
no na faclan—a rèir d' acras
no d' ealain san dròbh.

Whoso list to hunt

You who like the plash
or netting the wind
I know where there's a hind

plebs like you won't ever hunt.
It's decked in diamonds:
I'm Caesar's—noli me tangere.

Bugger the prohibition,
go flighty in the dusk,
bend and loosen the rope

and take the deer off, or the words—
as befits your hunger
or your skill at mart.

Peter Mackay

Boris's Tea Towel

Boris, you finally *'Got Brexit Done'*
and you've put your scone on a tea towel
just to let everyone know you've won, we've moved on, gone.
You can put your triumphal boat on the Queen's coin
so to have a rave, dance on half a country's grave
on Jezza's, Teresa's and your old mate Dave's.
A tea towel a very cheap domestic trick
another spin suggestion from the devil Dominic?
A sly way of being in with the Nation's kitchen bricks.

So why not go the whole hog,
put your fizzog on paper in the bog?
Then we could wipe your smug face on our arses,
allow us to reach a kind of catharsis
when we go for an extremely hard Brexit.
For you Prime Minister it's worked out well
but your face on a tea towel, wow, that's really lame.
At the end of the day when it goes Tom Tit Hell
you and Farage, we'll all know who to blame.

Julian Colton

Truth

Truth
is a sword
with more than one edge
one
side
can
wound
the
other
can
cut
the
ties
and
set
us
free

Kate Lindsay

The Economist and I

the economist and I are frae the same lang toun
he was shaped by the capital and spending time with Hume
inspired patriot rebels and came to influence soon
everyone from Marx to Wall Street tycoons
I was there in the nineties, before dial-up was obsolete
when the fans in the railway stand used to fill all the seats
the settled will of the people, for some remained incomplete
half-time in Munich and they'll be dancing in the streets
more than 200 years after the philosopher's death
with his statues and institutes and the national debt
even a far-off asteroid bears his fabled epithet
like a Champagne Supernova from my cousin's cassette
and the fireworks above his theatre which made me upset
an explosive debate surrounds his key messages
like Jacobite rebellions and yes-voting percentages
hearing Brimful of Asha on the Forty-Five carriages
of the fairground dodgems recalled in fragmentary images
these Links Market memories and a free market idol
cited when 'greed is good' experienced a revival
but would it be sacrilege or breaking with protocol
to suggest the hand's invisible cause is not there at all?

'read the whole book', some dissenters would say
insisting he foretold industrial misery and drudgery
and saw vast inequality wherever there's great property
not like some zealot for the modern gig economy
if division of labour can make us happy and smarter
it won't be when my leisure time means you have to work harder
that's the dogma of Thatcher and most Presidents post-Carter
to pursue one's own ends with a furious ardour
while some live in opulence and others in destitution
the homeless man told me about a cultural revolution
that we should all be feminists like Chimamanda's solution

this is bigger than Asis Ansari, it's entrenched in institutions
so if men are jacks of all trades, but masters of none
it means we're all responsible, but monsters not one
before the enlightenment the real witch-hunts were run
women burned at the stake now left to rot in the sun
reject the tabloid hysteria and see the pattern of causation
they bragged of spit-roasting sluts during grand slam celebrations
she faced a blaze of sceptics, they were cleared of all the allegations
what does that say about the health of our sick nations?

some things matter more than the wealth of our six nations
where flaming schemes engulf kids' dreams and some of them go unfed
they get sympathy till they're twelve, then they're just called neds
my Gran knew her butcher and baker, she goes to Tesco now instead
'place them in the bagging area' is all that anyone said
through self-interest not benevolence, these exchanges became unfettered
it's insincere to scaremonger, but some things could be better
we're all looking for the next prophet, the next hero or trendsetter
just remember that the postie is equal to the man of letters

Callum Macdonald

To Sorley Maclean

'The dead have been seen alive'
                              (Hallaig)

Didn't I see him, the Kensalyre miler,
my own grandfather, on global TV
in the blood-soaked vest of Macedonia
or some such doomed nation with high hopes revived?
Just as great John MacLean of your clan marches
through other broken streets, loved and despised,
holding untouchable hands in Bihar.
While the fighters for Spain are women in black,
straight their backs, bent their heads like your wood,
but black, of birches, holding vigils for peace
in Israel/Palestine. They have been seen.
Not only in Screapadal of your people,
not only in Strath of my grandfather's,
where the wind still has a clear run, carrying
spores of your birches and hazels like migrants
over the sea. Like your Highland woman
who's missed the boat in Tirana but is alive,
so to see, wiping green bile from her baby's mouth.
The ruins of the black houses are dead still
but cloud vapour forms endlessly, reforming
and surviving. Like the knock-kneed martyr
of the African desert —unseen, unsung
by all but you— the unadorned Englishman
who has now been seen on other cratered sand
where he clings to life and says God is Great.
The shadow he stands in is death's, not a rowan's,
but for the time being he's breathing fire.
In that way of seeing you too are alive,
white bardic hair blowing in the wind, singing
at the song-poem festivals of small nations

whose languages are like a wounded deer.
And your girl, not least, of the gold-yellow hair
seen again and again from Johannesburg
to Caracas, the hair dappled with dark dust
in the shanty towns or brighter than bright
on global TV. And she brings us to bear
all that which I've no name for but Hallaig,
or to forget it, the blackness, in our days too.

Edward Mackinnon

British Bulldogs

It's not the numbers but their strength
of will. They stand in rows across the hall,
determination in their posture, certainty
in the way they plant their feet, form fists.

It's these you must encounter, run towards
as if there wasn't a tomorrow, only yesterdays
they believe in, you do not. A whistle blows,
crowds of you surge forward, seek a gap.

It's true some make it through to safety
at the far end of the gym. Others, not so lucky,
scurry sideways, flounder, give in to their fate.

It's over in these moments. Force and bluster
gain the day. What hope there was is dashed
in sweat, the panting outcome of the game.

Brian Johnstone

Climate Change March

I walk along the cliff
on the day of the march.
No penance this
to watch the breakers
scudding in below,
to smell the tang
of salt-spangled grasses.

In the cities people
jostle together
spewing out hot air,
Instagramming selfies
from their blood-diamond phones.
Do they all *walk* there?

And will they eat neeps and tatties
from down the road,
give up their avocados?
Will we stop burning out
our eyes and the national grid
with our computer screens?

It's historic, says my friend,
takes the train
hundreds of miles south.
As historic as Iraq
when millions marched
And they went to war anyway?

Hot sun in September.
Seasonal? Maybe...
Or maybe another ice floe
has melted
at the top of the world.

I move on the earth,
breathe in the wind.
On the path, a tiny mouse
lies trodden to death
by a clumsy human foot.

Jean Rafferty

An Interesting File

I am an interesting file
and my cover is brown human skin
the chosen colour wasn't my fault
but historically your media see it as sin
I am an interesting file
and my cover is brown human skin

It has a drawing of my thoughts
a scan of my fingerprints in every airport
and tears waiting for my loved one
I am an interesting file
or perhaps I am a suspect project
came from nowhere on a horse made out of mist
carrying invisible weapons
and yes I admit
all the bullets of your malice severely hurt my heart

I am an interesting file
or maybe I am a myth
a story of drunken death
followed by sniffing dogs
running down from your elitism
so send me the ugliness of your racism
to shroud the corpse of my dignity

Ghazi Hussein

Immigrants

A horde of Viking birds
        descends
                to pillage
                        our rowan trees.
They squabble
        in foreign accents
                feasting
                      and carousing.
Should we try to
        apprehend them?
                You say
                      'Send them back to Norway!'
But there are arguments
            for asylum—
                  foxes, eagles,
                        men with guns.
In detention
        should fieldfares
                be kept apart
                      from redwings?
Perhaps they are economic migrants
        just here for the berries
                moving on when
                      they have all gone?
Even the bullfinch agrees
        there was too much fruit
                this year
                      for the residents alone.
So we let them flock
        from tree to tree
                scot free
                      free as birds.

Mandy Haggith

Post-Christmas Carol

To be sung at the Feast of St Brexit

Jesus, Mary and Joseph
       arrived at the UK Border:
got locked inside a cage because
       their papers weren't in order.

The good church-going folk
       in the London parliament
had declared their sacred realm
       a hostile environment.

Jesus, Mary and Joseph
       got put in their place:
their skins clearly marked them as
       an inferior race.

. See the high-headyins,
       each lord and dame,
tell the Holy Family
       'Go back whence you came!'

Jesus, Mary and Joseph
       slept in bedding rife with bugs.
Folk said: 'Don't give them money—
       they'll just spend it on drugs.'

Month after month
       they heard language crass and crude:
Joseph remarked: 'At least wi Herod
       ye kent whaur ye stood.'

Tom Hubbard

Laundrette

The peeling paint, the dirty roughcast on the walls outside
glaring deprivation marked *Temple Laundrette*. A face in the window
made me glance again. Wan, carrying the weight of the world on her
shoulders, she looked out and our eyes met for a second.

Years spun away like the huge churning machine, grey clothes spinning, a young
immigrant with no place in a tiny flat,
with no washing machine carrying the bag of unwashed laundry
to a dark place like this one, was it *West End Laundrette*?

Worrying for the right change in her hands, holding new unfamiliar money,
watched in despair as the homesickness rose in her like the soapy foam
in the machine, cleansing away the old and folding in the new.
She turned away.
I did the same.

Leela Soma

Leavings

A total of 345 babies have been found dead in refuse heaps in Karachi, since the beginning of 2017. 98% are female. Volunteers from local charities bury them.

—Metro.com news, April, 2018

They choose to work in daylight, these men
who dig small graves. Witnessing
needs light. There's time to straighten
bird-boned limbs, smooth tissue-fine eyelids
to tender, final sleep; offer some sweetness
of prayers, sung as vain antidote. They know
of course, that nothing, *nothing* can lighten
what happened here in the dark.

Let's give them names, for in the haste to discard
no one blessed them with a name.
Asali ... made of honey, Azzaa ... gazelle, Shalma ... good natured,
Bahaga ... beautiful, Ateera ... fragrance like perfume, Jinani ... heavenly,
Zahriyya ... flower.
                        Beautiful, sweet, heavenly, graceful,
delicate, good-natured, fragrant babies. And find
more names. So many, many more.

Make certain though, of one bitter truth—
find girl-names, female-names. Don't insult them
with anything else. They died
because they were female-born. So name it.
At least give them that.

Sheila Templeton

The New Petite Bourgeoisie

They've come from the dark wasteland provincial streets,
boys and girls from Blackburn, Paisley, Manchester and Leeds.
They were once the underdog poor like you and me
but since they received their law degrees, went into IT,
become middle-class, the new petite Bourgeoisie.
Some moved down south to Brighton, London and Kingston-Upon-Thames,
see their new world order through a rose-tinted lens,
boys and girls from Preston, Glasgow, Birmingham and Tees.

Once listened to Marley, Cooper Clarke and Linton Kwesi—
in life everyone has to finally move on,
but turning your back, sneering at the people you came from?
Used to vote red Labour, now vote blue Tory,
boys and girls from Bradford, Ripon, Scarborough and Grimsby.

In the seventies protested sus laws and rioted,
many I considered my friends; some were hooligans but kind-hearted,
now think there should be controlled immigration
or 'an adult conversation about it.' Every box ticked.
Let's face it, these selfish bonehead bastards voted Brexit.
Don't believe me? Look at their postings on the internet,
totally different people with something to protect,
forget that like them others might wish to slip through the net.
Terrace and High-Rise roots decidedly shunned,
now their kids have a privileged private education,
these boys and girls from East Ham, Derby, Aberdeen and Wear.

Take three holidays a year and all the gym subscription gear,
make the school run in the gas-guzzler Four by Four,
say fuck to the environment and the underclass poor.
All across the land it's pension schemes, funeral plans,
demand lower rates and grey pound tickets for Glastonbury,
say screw public services like hospitals and libraries.
Now they've aspired, these greedy aged fools,
nostalgic for the old Empire and WTO rules,
they adore the Royals, love Boris and Trump, I'm truly appalled
at boys and girls from Longsight, Moss Side, Govan and St Pauls.

Julian Colton

Londres 38

I did not enter
cuffed blindfolded
eyes taped
under sunglasses

I did not wear
the clothes
stripped from corpses
rank with electric sweat

I did not learn
to tell the time
of day and night
by what the DINA ate

I did not bleed
from gums
spitting teeth
like orange pips

I did not flinch
when tools
wrenched fingernails
hammered ears deaf

I did not clamp
my tongue
as they flicked the switch
razorsliced my breast

I did not gag
on choking bile
from holding down
the names

I did not watch
my mother writhe
tied to the metal frame
sprung with rats

I did not hang
from fleshtorn feet
hooded head drowning
in excrement

I did not disappear.

Annie McCrae

Note—Londres 38 is a building in Santiago, Chile. From September 1973 until the end of 1975 it was used by the dictatorship-era secret police, the DINA, as a clandestine detention and torture centre.

An estimated 2000 people were illegally detained in the house. 98 were subsequently disappeared, including 14 women, two of whom were pregnant. Of the 98 victims, 64 were members of the Revolutionary Left Movement (MIR), 81 of the 98 were under 30 years old, and eight were under 20. Of the four major clandestine torture centres in Santiago it is the only one that was not destroyed and has been reclaimed as an active memory site open to the public.

Geographical Exclusions Apply

to hear the Gaelic ann an taigh–mòr
air a' chrìoch eadar dà shiorrachd
ann an Èirinn far am faighear taic
o gach comhairle gus na dìogan a ghlanadh,
na claisean a chàradh, ged nach robh e
idir gu leòr agus fios gun teagamh sam bith
gun robh an taigh á grodadh, nach bi
e fada son t-saoghail seo, leis gun robh e—
mar gach taigh-mòr eile—á tuiteam
às a chèile on mhullach, gun robh
na sglèatan á crochadh air adhar,
na cabair phreasach nas làine de thuill
na de dh'fhiodh 's it was lovely to hear
the Gaelic aig solas dearg ann an Gleann
Comhann far an do stad car agus shlaighd
fear sìos an uinneag agus leig e às—
gu slaodach—cnap cotain a bha stobte
sa bheul ann am beàrn far am b' àbhaist
fiacal a bhith, an cotan air tionndadh
dearg gorm dubh agus air maistrich
le na duilleagan's an traillich's an uisge
ronnach ruadh á ruith sios á chlais
sìos dhan it was lovely to hear the Gaelic
anns á chlò á chlò á chlò às am bi
fàileadh an eilein-sa ag èirigh gach trup
a bhios tu fàs teth agus fliuch aig an aon àm
mar gum b' e comharra feise a bh' ann
rud cho borb bèisteal's nach urrainn dhut
a chumail ri taobh do chraicinn, nad
achlaisean, eadar do shlèistean, gun iad a bhith
air an suathadh, air an sgròbadh a bhith dearg
's dubh 's geal 's tu ag ràdh eadar fiaclan dùinte
an ceann a chèile Moire Moire Moire it was

lovely to hear the Gaelic aig àm dol fodha
na grèine, gus am bris an là, air là buidhe
Bealltainn, aig mullach na creige ann an Gippsland
far an do shad an Sgitheanach
Aonghas Mac á Mhaolain tùsanaich
far an oir dèidh peilearan
a chur nan casan mar gurn b' e plàigh
a bh' annta neo beathaichean leòinte
nach robh fiù's airidh air tròcair,
nach b' unnta ach trocan it was lovely
to hear the Gaelic air an t-seann sgeir,
na glasan-làimhe a' bìdeadh d' abhbrannan
's do chaoil-dhùirn agus an t-sàl
a' suathadh d' fheòla agus an reothart
a' lìonadh gun dòchas agad—agus i
an àm a' phreasaidh a-rithist an-còmhnaidh
mar a bha ' s mar a bhitheas, cha neònach e—
ach guth fir thar nan tonn a' dùrdail it was lovely

Geographical Exclusions Apply

to hear the Gaelic in a big house
on the border between two counties
in Ireland where you could get help
from both councils for cleaning the gutters,
repairing the roads, even though it was
never enough and there was no doubt
that the house was rotting, not long
for this world, since it was—like every other
big house—tearing itself apart
from the top down, and the slates
were hanging in air and the corrugating
roofbeams more full of holes than wood
and it was lovely to hear the Gaelic at a red
light in Glencoe where a car stopped and a man
wound down his window and dropped—
gently—a sop of cotton that had been
stoppering a hole in his mouth where once
there'd been a tooth, the cotton now turning
red blue black and swirling chewing
masticating with the leaves and butts
in the red rusted water running down the gutter
towards it was lovely to hear the Gaelic
in the tweed the tweed the tweed from which
the smell of this island rises each time
you get both hot and wet at the same time
as if it was a marker of sex, something so
barbaric and animal you could not keep it
beside your skin, in your armpits, between
your thighs without them being rubbed
and scratched red and black and white
while you say between teeth gritted together
Mary Mary Mary it was lovely to hear
the Gaelic at the going down of the sun, when the day

breaks, till the day of the moon, at the top
of the cliff in Gippsland where the Sgitheanach
Aonghas Mac a' Mhaolain threw aborigines
over the edge, having shot them in the legs
as if they were a plague, or wounded
animals, that weren't worthy of pity
that were nothing but brutes it was lovely
to hear the Gaelic on the ol' tidal rock
the manacles biting into your ankles
and wrists and the brine of the rising
spring tide seasoning your flesh and
no hope left but—it being the time
of the press-gangs again, as usual,
as it was and shall be, there are no surprises—
a male voice murmuring over the waves it was lovely

Peter Mackay

lyra mckee

it was a full moon on the creggan the night she died

overlooking the long tower
the shirt factories
the brandywell

she was a journalist
not one of them, one of us

she was one of us

some say it was a 'ra guy
some say it was a yobbo out to make a name

but hers is the name that will be remembered
not forgotten like the factory girls

or the yobbo

Colin Rutherford

Isefra Itwattun

We stood, up on the hills of our own destiny,
denied our own rights,
fulfilled with mystic identity
upon the hills of your wisdom,
a scream for liberty, from death to eternity.

On the land of *imussnawen*,
myths, tales of wisdom fighting oblivion,
summits of your high hills,
life of spoken reality.

A voice of existence, upon existence hymn,
written symbols of our own history
for the poor and powerless souls,
the definitive survival and continuity.

In the mountains forgotten by god,
only our philosophy can bring solace.
Such deep truths powerfully prevail
from the invisible words of forgotten poetry.

Mazigh Buzakhar

Isefra Itwattun in Amizig/Berber means 'The Forgotten Poetry'
Imussnawen in Amizigh/Berber means 'Wise men'

Land of no God

In the land of no breath,
no sense and no art.

There are many times
we are lost.

Hit by winds of hypocrisy
in the fog of *Tikerkast*.

Many can remember,
many are ready to die.

Lost again, with no hope,
surviving a life
of survived words.

You wrote pages of existence;
no creations, no history, no ideas.

Away from forgetfulness,
away from the dark side.

Gone again,
lost in the land of no god.

Mazigh Buzakhar

Tikerkast in Amizigh/Berber means 'lies or fake words'

Homonym Plunder

with foe piety
they pray upon us
these profits of death
these bottom-line martials
who make the rich idols
while the poor suffer a loan
and suffer always alone
caged in a sell
ate daze a weak
losing hour minds
as the mighty eight the week
oh, how they whined and they dined
and licked every last peace
with our bodies on a steak
and our blood read as meat
the world's now in vein
as the son starts to brake
on the seize of the land
on the cracks on our souls
on the waits on our feat

Callum Macdonald

Dangerous Time

It's when those who went through it get old and die,
when the liars come forth and say it was a hoax,
tell you your conspiracy theory was right all along.

We talk sensibly over supper, two adult generations
sparring, laughing—one that has grown up with
only profit and markets, that finds our *old hippiness* naive.

We are good people, we have never known war or want,
so we are reasonable, tolerant, we listen to argument,
but we have not lived each other's lives, so we doubt.

And I am tired of hoping, afraid to die without testimony
of a benign politics; afraid of the posts, chatlines, the websites
that say it was a lie, a hoax; fake and false and facetious.

Vivien Jones

Common Rebels

On a shipping pallet with only a blanket
to cover the straw, softening
the pressure of shoulder, hip, knee and ankle bones,
hard and cold against this makeshift bed.
Live-in protestors
undercover
of plastic slung across a rope
between two trees,
we slept under the stars.

Since 'Embrace the Base' in '82
the Greenham Common protest
had become women only.
Taking leave of homes to make peace,
our farewells bereft of triumphal brass bands
and flag-waving well-wishers.

Instead, home comforts were traded
for never knowing when the bailiffs
and the police would come,
often at night to evict,
blinding our half-awake eyes with their torches
while we shone a light on their unquestioning logic.

They dragged us about, forcibly
removing our tents and sleeping bags
and singling out those they saw
as the ring leaders for special treatment,
in the hope they would grind us all down.

Or that the vigilante groups who were never caught,
armed with buckets of maggots, blood,
pig manure and fireworks
                              or just their fists
would carry on their dirty work.

When they could catch us first.

For we took it in turn, on the night watch.
Sending signals around the base, from
the yellow to blue to green and violet gates.
Bundling what we could along with ourselves
into our waiting vans.

Then returning to the Common
once they'd gone.
Singing: *You can't kill the spirit...*
and debating, our many and divergent politics
as we wove a world of different possibilities.

Subverting femininity, we laid our bodies down
again and again as blockades,
against the workers arriving to build the silos
to keep the missiles safe.

The Secretary for Defence told Parliament
we would never get into any sensitive areas
but women danced on the silos that New Year's Eve
and just weeks later, three occupied Greenham's
air traffic control tower for hours.

As April arrived, teddy bears scaled the perimeter
fence to hold a picnic
and mirrors were held up to the police around
and the British military just inside the base
to reflect back, the onslaught they justified
in the name of *following orders.*

When the missiles eventually arrived
women tore down miles and miles of fence
and over the years
were arrested for trespassing, time and again.

On one such night, under a sickle moon in '85
we crept close, keeping watch for the soldiers to pass
until our bolt cutters snipped our entrance.

Hand in hand, we strode toward the nuclear warheads
and in a flash the American military, deep at the heart
of the matter, surrounded us.

One pointed a sub-machine gun at my pregnant belly,
warning me to stop or he might shoot,
then he tutted and shook his head as he asked:
Does your husband approve
of you being out here doing this?

I kept walking toward the silos and enquired:
Does your mother approve of you pointing a gun
and threatening to kill women and children?

As we walked on, he began to back-track,
calling for police reinforcements to arrest us.

We were processed in a portacabin
doubling as a police station
for the local prison was full
of Greenham wimmin

who, one way or another, kept the protest going
till the last cruise missile had gone in 1991.
Some are still going strong.

Lesley Benzie

Note—Gorbachev explicitly mentioned Greenham women when he said that the European peace movement enabled his decision in 1986 to meet Ronald Reagan, leading to the INF Treaty.

Only in a Commonweal

A Chorus of Labour against Capital

Where the chains of Capitalism are forged,
there they must be broken...

—Rosa Luxemburg

We are the nothings you walk past.
Your lowest and least,
we live in the margins of your power.
Expendable, we fight your many wars.
Your triumphs we pay for, but have none.

Unheeded and unnamed,
we make your schemes come true.
Every sweated brick and girder, every milligram and tonne
of every building you command is ours.
Every furrow ploughed and filled with seed is ours.
Your wealth-producing factories, your cities—ours!

Day in, day out, we do your work and will.
We pipe the water that you need
from reservoir to tap; we stitch the clothes
that cover up your nakedness;
we bake the bread (and cake) you eat.

We are your numerous and essential kin.
Suffering most, we learn most.
Our slave-songs make symphonies;
our longings, creeds.

We dig your graves.

David Betteridge

If only Nicholas Witchell spoke Scots

Am fair scunnered wi the hail lot o them
an wi the hail nonsense o it aw.
This latest stooshie is the last straw fur me
wi they wee pups sayin they've hud enuff
an wantin tae be *'financially independent.'*
Aye, right! That will be right so it will.
They've baith got heaps o siller as it is
an whit they want, whit they really want
is tae mak mair oan the celebrity circuit
talkin a load o posh pish tae whaever peys
the maist. She'll probly bring oot a wee scent
cawd *'Miss Markle'* or *'Markle's Sparkle'* or the like
an he's got his games tae craw aboot
alang wi some bits an pieces o charity wurk
coz the richer they ur the mair they luve charity.

But it's no jist thon, it's his bluidy faither Cherlie.
He cannae thole me an ah cannae thole him,
an as fur that drunken blellum that's his faither's wife
an his dodgy uncle Andy wi yon yank that's twistit
an his ither uncle Eddie naebdy seems tae talk aboot
an the auld duke that's jist aboot tae keel ower
an his granny whae jist winnae ivir keel ower
til her faimly is the richest yin oan the face o the earth—
ach, ah've hud enuff o the hail lot o them
wi aw ma snivvelin an crawlin efter them
wi ma sappie voice like Holy Willie afore me
when maist folks jist huv tae get by as best they can
an some o them cannae dae that wi zero oors
an huv tae go tae foodbanks tae keep it aw thegither
fur aw that an aw that am gonnae be —a republican!

Jim Aitken

I saw a new world being assembled

In the tenements
there were workers
who built dreams for others

singers who got drunk
on rebel songs
fighters who fought

for themselves
in the workplace
and lost every round

all in revolt
against an assembly line
of masters

I saw a new world
being assembled
in a sweatshop

where dreamers
singers and fighters
unfurled a trade union flag

their voices bolted
and welded into one

Owen Gallagher

ELSEWHERE

austerity with government—sanctioned glee aims
a sniper rifle at their foreheads

—Magi Gibson from 'Our Boys'

I am not here, then, as the accused: I am here as the accuser of capitalism
dripping in blood from head to foot.

—John MacLean at his sedition trial, 9 May 1918

Pu' Scotland up,
And wha can say
It winna bud
And blossom tae.

—Hugh MacDiarmid, *A Drunk Man Looks at the Thistle*

Wishing—Not—Well

Whatever the opposite of merit is
they surely have it:
the manipulators, the moulders of opinion
and their lackeys and lickspittles —
the career-men and sleekit hangers on,
guzzlers at the trough.

I lie awake
and wish them—oh, not well. Yet school myself
to thinking they have the reward
of living with their own pure ugliness
until they die, which may not come
soon enough

but sooner, I hope, than for the poor folk, oldies
who totter on zimmer frames,
the women on the bus, the single mums
with fractious kids
or the rough sleepers in doorways
who wait and hope and drop, because they must.

Donald Adamson

Swinging on the State Gibbet

they used to hang people at the crossroads
leave the body to rot until a skeleton
a warning of state retribution

there was a trial and a jury
so that the poor who stole to live
were not denied summary justice—from above

they used to export the unhanged
exiled to hard labour
fodder of a new world
the fruits of their work to be repatriated
but never their shadow

now there are DWP assessments
without need for jury
skeletons lie on pavements and in doorways
to warn of state judgement

no requirement to send away to hard graft
zero hours contracts and work till you die
casualties of a new economic order
isolate the labourer from all riches
no comfort of home

at each crossroads on the path to wealth
a cold wind blows
rattles the bones

George Colkitto

The City

Hope has not broken out,
to the East of the city.
In the distance, we
hear the sirens, men
in uniforms, coming
to close off the streets,
to barricade the families
into their homes, and
spray paint the black
crosses of contagion
            on their doors.

And, of course, we have seen all this before.

Young men, poisoned by
hope, dream of peace,
and cannot be made to
be soldiers. They are no
use to the generals and
must be shut away
behind fences, where
they wander, eyes always
open, gazing sightlessly
at the fatal premise,
that the world might,
otherwise, not be like
            this.

And, of course, we have seen all this before,
        we have lived through this before.

In the infirmaries
nurses move silently
between the beds, ears
sealed with adhesive
tape—in case some
hopeful word, some
thought, some idea
escapes from a patient's
mouth and crawls,
undetected, up the
brain-stem and into
the un-inoculated
stations of their
            minds.

And, of course, we have seen all this before,
    we have lived through this before,
        we have suffered all this before.

Families, infected by
hope, believe the rumours
about clean water and fall
victim to cholera or typhoid.
They talk—in the marketplace
or by the school, where parts
of children are laid out, for
identification and collection
—about a vaccination against
hope, a single injection to
palliate the agony of belief,
that someday, their lives will
be lived outside of this
            perimeter of ruins.

And, of course, we have seen all this before,
we have lived through this before,
we have suffered all this before
—and
we have learned

Without hope, we may live.

Chris Boyland

Bee Division

Those bees are inferior
their emerald posteriors
mark them as insects of fun
their offspring are smelly
they steal Royal jelly
and fritter about in the sun.
Throw them out of the hive!
Why should they be alive
when their betters are working,
no concept of shirking?
You finish the task you've begun.

Orange bees are élitist
their honey's the sweetest
and hives are much neater than most
but their efforts are vain
if their life's greatest aim
is to complement somebody's toast.
Our philosophy's clear
so let's wanton my dear—
pollinate the wild clover
where fuchsia hangs over
the streams and the glens and the coast.

I'm the hexagon Queen
and I rarely have seen
such devotion and service and craft.
The orange are pretty
the emerald are witty
but sometimes I think they're all daft.
Their kith and their kind
are all left behind
by the Royals and gentry
who wing it on plenty
and generally have the last laugh.

Anne Connolly

Nostalgia Revisited

Cat owners used to second best
Whose preferences were unexpressed;
Kids who never felt quite full,
Unglowing on the trek to school;
Girls whose eyes would scour bookshelves,
Not dote on dolls that wet themselves;
Women who weren't content to sing
And dance while doing the vacuuming...
The glamour of that lost decade
Covers up the faded, frayed,
Or else just differently prized:
Our lives were not as advertised.
Think, while the New World Symphony
Plays over homespun poverty:
This was the liveliness of youth
You must now substitute with truth.

David Cameron

Unskilled

Eftir Charles Simic

De aks fir a tully-knife
I come runnin
dey need a lamb
I interduce mesel as da lamb

Dir aafil vexed
it seems dey need some rat-pooshin
an dey need a crofter
fir der flock o tarantulas

A'm blyde A'm browt me
blood-sokkit letters o interdiction
me weel-thoomed daeth certeeficate
signed and stampit

Dir gotten a crex an a fivver
if I staand idda greff fur dem
in me mort-cloot smookie
a'll be weel hanselled da moarn

Bit dir cheenged der minds ageen
noo dey want a sangbird, in voar
an dey want a wife
ta sopp an sluice dir pillies

O I kin dae dat tö I say
absolutely nae budder avaa
tweetin an cheepin lik a lintie
spreadin da sheeks o me erse

Jim Mainland

dey, they; dir, they are/they have; vexed, very sorry; blyde, pleased; crex, cough, idda greff, (fig.) in the front line; mort-cloot, shroud; smookie, smock; hanselled, rewarded; voar, spring; pillies, penises

Credit where it is Due

So you breathe like Darth Vader and you walk like Yoda,
you're nearly dead but you can peddle Coca-Cola.
For fifty years of labour is never enough,
learn to email, peasant, or you'll be sleeping rough.

You served society and you think you served it well
but you still have a few breaths left and labour to sell.
So you get your arse on a bike, and look for a job,
cleaning toilets will make you feel part of the mob.

Minimum wage! You know I can't say fairer than that,
you may think I'm a pig but we all know you're a rat.
For an accident of birth is all that binds us,
that and bullshit stories to keep you on this bus.

I will only ever give credit where it is due,
show me a worker and I'll show you someone to screw.
Don't be shocked and awed by a bit of candour,
if it comes from your mouth we will call it slander.

John Tinney

We didn't know we were poor

We didn't know we were poor.
Boiled eggs chopped up in a teacup,
the warm yellow yolk pooling
over the white chunks;
white bread soldiers on a plate
a teaspoon to scoop the last morsels,

nothing to do with a lack of egg cups

We didn't know we were poor.
Mince and sausages, corned beef,
circular slices of pink ham,
lots and lots of filling mash and gravy,
jugs of runny custard, semolina,
rice pudding and rhubarb

a roasted chicken at Christmas

We didn't know we were poor.
My mother did; she filled all five of us
with scraps and leftovers, making a feast
of every meal, welcoming her hero home
with a set-aside dish—something spicy
for my father—we sniffed and frowned—

later, she ate the leftovers of ours.

Vivien Jones

Wasted

In ma hoose, if you'll pardon the exaggeration,
there's like ten billion bins in a million locations.
There's bins in each room and there's six bins tae spare,
even outside ma gaff there's three mair bins oot there.
A trio of wheelie bins, black, brown and blue,
which bin's oot on bin night I haven't a clue.
Bins so full of crap it defies explanation,
bins that need sorted oot, to ma lastin vexation.

And where does it go, aw this thrown away shite?
Whit happens tae waste oot of mind, oot of sight?
Can we rest in oor beds, thinkin that we've done right,
havin done oor wee bit for auld Mother Earth's plight?

Sad fact is that loads of it's shipped overseas,
in corporate deals done wi the greatest of ease.
Chuck it intae a landfill and make a quick buck,
cause you know that big businesses don't gie a fuck.
Aye, there's cash tae be made and a profit tae squeeze,
wi the rich getting richer by cutting doon trees.
Deid sea-life washed up wi their guts full of plastic,
a sign of good business, a killing fantastic.

But it seems aw the poor folk are shit out of luck,
Mother Earth's fuckin ragin and runnin amuck.
The winters get colder, the summers hotter,
rivers so full of trash you could walk on the water.
Aw, that one clip on Youtube that curled ma toes,
that straw getting yanked oot that wee turtle's nose.
As it screamed, bled and thrashed in its terrified throes,
aye, it's man's cruel dominion, Ah sadly suppose.

But the waste of the world could be reused again
to make playgrounds with slides, chutes and swings for the weans.
We could use aw that plastic to pave and maintain
all oor highways and byways, it's fuckin insane.
Aw the big plastic bottles? Make clothes for the cold,
plastic jaickets and fleeces in numbers untold.
Plastic 3-D print homes wi plastique window panes,
so the folks without hooses don't sleep in the rain.

When from thrown away trash so much good could be wrought,
we could remake the world if we gave it some thought.
Aye, the worst waste of all are our God-given brains,
whit bam burns their ain hoose for the monetary gains?

D.A. Watson

Ìobairt 2001

Tha an t-earrach seo tostach,
gun sprèidh air an raoin,
gun mhèillich chaorach
no freagairt uan,
gun chrodh is laoigh ruadha
a' breacadh nan slios
ach an casan spàgach
gan stiùireadh ri nèamh,
am brùthan cruinn torrach
a' brùchdadh san teas,
toit dhubh am feòla
a' cur ìmpidh air an t-Sannt.

Sacrifice 2001

This spring is dumb
without stock in the fields,
without the bleating of ewes
and answering lambs,
without cows and their calves
giving colour to the hills,
but their splayed legs
thrust to the skies,
their full wombs
bursting in the heat,
the black fumes of their flesh
petitioning Greed.

Meg Bateman

Meaning?

Iraq 2003

Collateral damage. Shock and Awe.
Where are the meanings that we had before?
Gives language a bad name does war.

Shock was his shaggy mane of hair until now,
a dozen corn sheaves stacked together
in a field. Something you 'got a bit of,' how
did it come to mean this nightly slaughter
every tooth in the city shaken?

And awe? Crouched under amputations
of falling glass—do they wonder
at those sublime illuminations
that rip homes and schools from under
them when 'targets' are mistaken?

Collateral—now there's a word misspent.
no longer money pledged against a loan,
but children burned alive
in the bent wreckage of a car. A hand blown
from a wrist. Splashed brains. Backs broken.

Collateral damage. Shock and Awe.
Where are the meanings that we had before?
Gives language a bad name does war.

Chrys Salt

Thorns

Did you ever see that fairy tale?
The one with the girl
with the shitty attitude?

Every time she opens her mouth
out come frogs and snakes and spiders.
It's hard to listen

to someone standing there
up to their thighs in spiders.
I see you know what I'm on about,

you've spat out a few frogs in your time.
Jeezo, they're disgusting.
You've tried to talk about, say, Tories,

but pulled midges from your lips
covered in spit.
I'm owning it, I'm going for thorns,

they can catch a little but
whose lips aren't a mess
this time of year?

I reckon if we all
focus together on brambles
we could build the kind of wall

that Trump would be after.
One of them with barbs and spikes
and long interlocking branches,

maybe some roses too.
Whatever.
Let the handsome princes

come galloping by.
I don't know about you but I reckon
I've got a hundred years of thorns in me.

Cara L. McKee

A Wide Berth

Hashtag stitches hem his cheek
back together, betraying a tender-hearted
childhood in soft-sunned playgrounds.

This is not the neighbourhood
from which he came
with its jagged-toothed windows,
perpetual car sirens, and daylight exorcisms
by the duck ponds;
Scotstoun's forlorn knighthoods.

He shivers awake, back seat into car boot.
Frosted tangerine is stapled on glass.
A blanket of taxing worry
is prised to shockwave brow,
savouring fevers for heat
and premature birdsong like daydreams.

Boats thawing snow dupe ducks
into believing bread has been thrown
but he is too long in the tooth.
Quick-stepping joggers' headphones
purr whispers from his lax youth
but cardboard prayers
translate tinny tunes
into hymns and gospel truth;

the opportunity to stop, think
and improve.

Stephen Watt

Beginning with a Photograph

I find you in early morning awakenings,
mute moments that wither
into the bustling places of the day.
The cemetery has been ploughed over.
Informal memories of the deceased ignore
uncounted ways of interrupting
accidents of time.

I find you in the intermediate spaces.
A gently smiling person gazes,
a visitor from unremembered pasts,
and children come to play. They bring secrets;
the desires they seek are not theirs
as each hopeful beginning realigns
in the margins of the playroom.

They linger, alien remainders
in our daily lives, inhabiting minds,
ghosts in our grandmother's eyes.
They rupture connections,
adorn rooms, fill gaps in family spaces,
asking when they will be
no longer missing.

Geraldine Gould

With thanks to Sue Lieberman's essay 'Missing', published in Emotion, Space and Society *(2015) exploring the effects of the Holocaust on generations who feel the absences and silences of distant ancestors.*

The Blacklist

Everyone sped off at the end of their shift.
No one saw him sobbing in his car.
No one paused to say he deserved a star
for speaking out; that his courage was a gift.

He feared his wife's reaction to the news,
he'd been sacked instantly without pay,
and was on a blacklist for his views,
this was his last working day.

No one saw him reverse his car
into the river and drop out of sight.
His workmates sent a sympathy card.
His wife set his boss's car alight.

Owen Gallagher

The Voices

The voices arrived every morning.

In fact, I often awoke to their jibber-jabber.
They weren't the voices of anyone I knew,
despite the intimacy they assumed.
They weren't people who would normally
have anything to do with the likes of me.

The way I heard it, there were four or five
of them in rotation. There was one harrumphing
male voice. He was very self-important.
He liked inviting other voices into the discussion
and then interrupting them, talking over them.
Occasionally, there were voices he did approve of.
He would let them talk to their heart's content
and even chuckle along with them.

Pretty soon his voice became intolerable to me.

Then there was a posh-sounding woman's voice.
And a male voice which spoke in blandishments.
The other voice —also belonging to a man—
was very chirpy and bumptious.

These voices all sounded very knowledgeable
about the world and well furnished with opinions.
They were always well pleased with themselves
and didn't have to take things too seriously
because whatever they had decided to talk about
wasn't likely to affect them personally.
It was all a bit of a laugh. If you get too serious
about things, well, that was a bit off, really.

There was one emotion they very much favoured,
but it was only available to a select few.
This was the emotion that was intrinsic
in the act of being 'moved' by something.
There seemed to be an unspoken consensus
as to what merited this accolade.
If something was deemed to be 'moving'
then it was highly acceptable and sought-after,
but not discernible by the multitude.

I soon got the impression that they presumed
I automatically shared their view of the world.

It was very difficult to ignore these voices.
I could only train myself to nullify them.
I noticed that if I listened closely,
what they were saying was utterly vacuous.
They simply repeated the same things,
in tired and unimaginative language,
in worn-out tropes and wearying platitudes.
If they accidentally hit upon a concept
that was new to them, they were flummoxed.
So they made sure they never did.
Anything that existed outside their own narrow
understanding of the world, as it had been
handed down to them, was mocked—
a defence mechanism, I suspected,
employed to cover their own insecurity.
No attempt was made to respond in depth.
Perhaps they feared I would no longer listen
if they didn't skip from one superficiality to the next.

Yet even when I managed to stop hearing them
I kept hearing them in a way because at other times
it was terribly easy to tune into the same
kind of things being said
again and again
in slightly different but eerily similar voices.

And so it happened that I found myself pitying
their little egos. Their forced smiles.
Their ersatz bonhomie. Those awkward times
when they tried to *'get down with the kids.'*

And I was suddenly suffused with despair,
realising that I could never help these plaintive,
disembodied voices, these hopeless, hapless burblings
of a decaying class trapped in some endless theatre
of the absurd
of their own making.

Jim Mainland

Feather

One rare day he saw
from the cell window, a feather drift,
no longer than his finger tip.

Only a small feather and
a small thought.
Only the smallest word.

Blessings on the birds,
each a memory of freedom.
Each has a right to its feathers.

I have a right to remember
the tanks in the square, the poem
I wrote. The smallest feather

too small to be found and jailed,
too light to be caught.

Kate Armstrong

Charity

Is this a holy thing to see
In a rich and fruitful land
Babes reduced (sic) to misery
Fed with cold and usurous hand?

—'Holy Thursday', *Songs of Experience*, William Blake

Two hundred years and more since the hosier's son
heard in children's voices dashing against
St Paul's impervious marble the *trembling cry*
of the poor, who would always be poor
until the New Jerusalem was built.

Two hundred years and voices rise again
into the dome of a lavish concert hall
alive with flags and misconstruction
where well-fed citizens, fattening the chorus,
howl for their *arrows of desire.*

Two hundred years and a young mother
queues in a draughty hall for a can of beans,
a packet of tampons, her fretful toddler
squirming against the straps of a hand-me down buggy,
his cheeks pale as winter, while down the street

a man whose age is half what his face tells us
pulls close his leaky sleeping-bag against
December's bluster, rattles the three small coins
in his plastic cup, Christmas lights tremble
and festive muzak circles well-filled aisles

thronged with last-minute shoppers.
Two hundred years. *So many children poor.*
Two hundred years, the nation *rich and fruitful*
treble times over—and I haver between
tinned custard and peach halves for the Foodbank collection.

A. C. Clarke

Conform or Die

There are the ordinary people,
they are always around you
so stand up, don't be shy now,
come on and take a bow.
In the court of average living,
standing on display like a prize fish,
your oddity is catch of the day—
on the menu, you're the main dish.

In the twilight hours of captivity
as you stare at the moss in the walls
you wonder with the steady drip of water
from the ceiling how this came to be.
Trying to hold flimsy memories in hand,
a tragic obscurity mockingly calls,
the moss seems to pulse radioactive,
colour bursting before tired eyes.

The last night ends with a bright dawn,
heralding a conclusion to an era of pain
as you are pulled by self- designed bondage
unceremoniously thrust into truth's light.
You are left with one choice, the last choice,
the greatest to ever be made—
to give in or continue to fight,
to conform or die.

Bee Parkinson-Cameron

we're not supposed to

we're not supposed to
be feral children
happy to wander the streets of our talents

we're not supposed to
walk
on the road where the cars go

we're not supposed to
talk
to the police in the wrong strong tone

we're not supposed to
disrespect
millionaires' private property

we're not supposed to
tune
into the news from *Russia Today*

we're not supposed to
get
drunk until we're sent to jail

we're not supposed to
take
control of our beautiful souls

we're not supposed to
steal
the wigs from balding judges

we're not supposed to
appear
on *Star Trek The Next Generation* or *Big Bang*

we're not supposed to
outlive
lazy lords who call themselves farmers

we're not supposed to
caress
our lovers with toil-weary hands

we're not supposed to
mark
life in seasons but only in storms

we're not supposed to
forget
to harvest an over-ripe crop

we're not supposed to
neglect
our couscous for tatties and rice

we're not supposed to
eat
excessive amounts of sugar and spice

we're not supposed to
extract
our own teeth with a dentist in sight

we're not supposed to
migrate
to the cities and steal the shit jobs

we're not supposed to
use
names like Charles or Harry or Grace

we're not supposed to
mock
the queen at Holyrood Palace

we're not supposed to
mock
the queen at Buckingham Palace

we're not supposed to
mock
the queen at Westminster Abbey

we're not supposed to
act
like we are above ourselves

we're not supposed to
remain
forever the lower orders

we're not supposed to
'live long and prosper'
as part of the infinite natural structure

we're not supposed to
be here any longer
yet here, here we are

—good night!

Jim Ferguson

Hauntin a toilet

The bonnie young polis, o I heard it aa
but plain claes wark was a chance tae get on

an I just had tae staun at this urinal
an be prepared tae sweir that's aa I done,

nae entrapment an nae encouragement,
OK ye didnae want tae pit them aff.

We liftit aa kinds. When the pubs came oot
at closing time the gents went like a fair,

there was a barracks then, the pits were open,
a miner said he seen my ears were burnin.

Ye got the hang o workin wi yir witness,
ye got the hang o that an guys confessed,

an no fir very lang was I the youngest
an whit had been a future came tae pass.

Gordon Dargie

Safe

safe as houses
she pretends
to remember
back in the '50s

safe as the weight
of her father's hand
felt on the back
of her legs

safe as some uncle
up from the country
saying she's nice
saying it twice

safe as the secret
she pretends to forget
she's always kept
safe as houses

Brian Johnstone

The Scottish Horse Squadron, Perth 1914

Oh aye we've looked
horses in the eye.
Those poor blinkered souls
sweat and tremble beneath men
like our country's women.
Mute creatures, bridled and led
into the fray of protest,
jostle shoulder to shoulder
against us as we sing outside
the prison today. Our voices will
be heard. We will get the vote, spit
the bit out from our mouths
but who speaks for them?

Finola Scott

Stories sans glory

The Great War for women was far away
their lives and limbs apart from the fray
sacrificing breadwinner, lover or son.

In World War II the joke would go:
Those who want to be a hero
add up to the sum of zero.
Those who want to be civilians
total somewhere in the millions.

Exploding to encompass billions,
safer soldier than civilian
World War lll will know no zones.

War zone women since the world was made
have gleamed on men's breasts on the victory parade.
Trophies, tributes, surrender tokens.

Trading for better or for worse
the master who in home tones cursed
for a lord whose commands were the snarl of a beast

Y chromosome labels you hero.
Double X the target below.

Mary McCabe

Wrong

I'm looking forward
being a father and
raising a little girl

I'm looking forward
to taking her out into
the world

I'm looking forward
to her first day at school
to explaining to her why
the white kids at school
don't play with the brown
kids, why the brown kids
get called names, why the
parents of the white kids
don't talk to the parents
of the brown kids, while
they're waiting at the gate.

I'm looking forward
to the day she learns
what judgment means

I'm looking forward
to reading her stories
about princesses and
castles and magic wands
and wishes that come
true, and explaining
to her why, at the end
of all the avenues of
wealth, there are people

sleeping on the street

I'm looking forward
to the day she learns
what money wants
and what it costs.

I'm looking forward
to going shopping, to
leading her down
the aisles of remedies
and promised perfection,
of all the paints and tints
and brushes, the nails and
clamps and hammers she'll
need to buy, to beat herself
into all the shapes she's told
are beautiful this week.

I'm looking forward
to the day she signs
her first prescription.

I'm looking forward
to decorating the room
in which she'll live,
papering the walls with
society's idea of who
she is and locking her
inside with nothing but
the opinions of people
who don't know her,
who have no idea what
she can be to keep her
safe at night.

I'm looking forward
to the day she learns
the sky is just a painted
ceiling, unless you're
born with the right sort
of wings.

I'm looking forward
to seeing her bottle
the very essence of
herself, cast it upon the
digital waves, watch it
bob away across the ocean
of connectivity and being
sent dick pics in return

I'm looking forward
to fitting her into the
prison of her white
dress, of pulling the
stays so tight she squirms
and complains that there's
no room in there to breathe

I'm looking forward
to saying to her, *'the
world thinks you were
made to suffer, little one
but I think you were made
to prove them wrong.'*

Chris Boyland

The Ludger

A'm fukkin fed up wi the ludger
he's been here far owre lang
oor hospitality's ae thing
but
this is a bit ower strang

it's no jist he aye gets
the pickin a awthin, whitivver we hae
but hoo we're supposit
tae stop shoutin
whan he's got something tae say

for shoutin's a natural habit
an argument like mither's breist milk
fer the fowk born intae
this hoose
a particklar, deep- thinkin ilk

an the thocht that these days
A'm thinkin
damn near aw the time
is
the ludger shuid gang
he's been here ower lang
an we cin tak back
thae things we nou lack
an tae fecht in the hoose
will be fine

Stuart McHardy

Look, I'm telling you I'm not angry

at the way you fell back in here at 3am,
pissed as a million farts. I'm not
angry that you dropped a fortnight's worth
of minging boxers, stinking socks and the rest
stunk on the floor, in the certainty
that you'd collect it, washed, hung and ironed. No.
I'm not angry that you've left
a manky plate, baked-on grime from the micro,
underneath your unmade bed. I'm
not angry that you treat this place
like a hotel, except no hotel would stand
for all this crap. I'm not angry
that your latest girlfriend looks at me
as if I've emerged from some midden,
even I try, really try to smile and wish
you'd find someone much more right. I'm
not angry that you've stomped off wordless,
worse, that you've told me where to go,
used terms no-one should ever
throw back at his mother. I'm not.

I'm angry that you've never had the chance,
in all your twenty years of life
to pit yourself against me,
cut my fifty seven years
of pretentions and conceit
down to size, make me think
of where my arch-shit stops.
I'm angry that all your needs
can never let you put me down.

Beth McDonough

In a once city of culture do pearls grow
(*grit in an oyster causes irritation which becomes a pearl*)

He sits in piss beneath the railway bridge,
asks for passing change of those in range
of his cracked voice.
Costa Coffee cup of loose coin
on the stained pavement
are his manna, his daily bread.
Four carrier bags, a whole
new view on what it meant
when they sold 'bags for life.'
These may well outlast him.
He is stretched, seams showing,
body abandoned.

She has a wheeled case.
Is crisply dressed for winter
as she stakes her place
with red sleeping bag.
Out of place, out of luck,
this is her Hilton, her flat, her future.
Above the London sleeper rumbles South,
others beginning their journey
with whisky in comfort,
as her brittle laugh greets her night
companions.

George Colkitto

A Candle for Stephen

It is fitting to think of you in here
to light a candle for the *Big Issue* seller
I got to know back in my own city
where I can recall our conversations on
the Blue Nile, your boyhood holidays in Sligo
and of your deep attachment to Glasgow Celtic.
There had been a happy enough childhood
before your brother died from a drug overdose
and provided you with the fatal attraction
that led directly to your own addiction
though you were clean for the last twenty years.
It is fitting to think of you in here
because of the millions of prayers that
have come from here, crept under the doors,
slid through the stained glass windows
out into the wider world and beyond
for all the living and for all the dead.
And the candle I lit for you flickers and rises
upwards, to where you surely are now.
Your story is being told in its flame
that will fade and then burn out
like all the other candles, like all the other
lives as well. But I silently watch it
and think of all your hopes and all your dreams
that seemed to keep you going, see you through.
You left an impressive impression on us all
with your determination, even when tired and wet
you kept it going, keeping your dreams alive
and your sense of humour made it easier
than it would otherwise have been.
And I will miss you, most certainly miss you
as the candle continues to burn and flicker
and as the burning injustice
of homelessness continues to inflame me.

Jim Aitken

Not Begging

An old tramp under a tree
not begging chained to a dog
asleep beneath a hawthorn
amongst his gathered goods
a pigeon nicking at his breid
tight wrapped in cellophane
spots of rain kept off by a golf
umbrella, lucky fella, this Crusoe
and no polis moving him on from
his patch outside Holyrood, Palace
and Parliament, not even two weeks
later, us got to nodding, and then
he's gone, and the hawthorn's barer
and me, reduced somehow, and poorer.

Alistair Findlay

The Third Street Along

The first street was the best,
a fandango of purple velvet frocks
and fearsome buckled boots,
an exuberant cocktail
of alternative retail and
retail alternatives.
Halfway up, the warmongering general
with the traffic cone on his head,
Glasgow's two fingered salute
to authority or high art,
or maybe both.

The Glasgow junkie moved in first,
face as grey and pocked as porridge,
gouching over his polystyrene cup
with its three copper coins.
Then the Romanian woman,
melodramatic in her pose
of abject supplication.
I had money then,
didn't mind paying a pound
to each of them.
It was the least I could do.

When it reached a fiver
to walk from one station
a hundred yards to the next,
I moved to the second street.
There was no-one there
at first. Bulging bin bags
on the pavement,
graffitied shutters and
side entrances to shops

up to the over-priced
fashion shop on the end.

Only two beggars came
to the second street,
a pink-faced woman
who'd once been an addict
and a dark-skinned man,
freezing in this northern city
so far from his home.
I had little money then,
gave fifty pence
to each of them.
It was all I could afford.

Now I stick to the third street
along, no-one there
but me, hurrying through
to the Victorian bar where cheap coffee
and cocktails belie chandeliered splendour.
I have no money now,
borrow to share drinks with my friends.
If the beggars come—and they will—
should I borrow money
to give to them?
Can I really walk past?

Jean Rafferty

Our Boys

They die, you know, left out on nights like this,
sleeping in shop doorways and in ditches,

foetal as uncurled ferns, dew-soaked at dawn.
What will you be when you grow up? That age old

question tossed their way when they were small,
playful as a bouncing ball. They learned to say:

lawyer, engineer, footballer, rich.
Now, they tease an early morning roll-up

between death-cold fingers. And in the no-jobs-here
Job Centre, plastic potted plants twitch

like dodgy camouflage when they appear,
the fluorescent light flickers its faulty detonator switch,

austerity with government-sanctioned glee aims
a sniper rifle at their foreheads, while battalions

of only-obeying-orders keyboards click click click
and the future slams the emergency exits shut.

Magi Gibson

grand for the hairst

having radically reached by radical foot
the radical summit of the radical hill
under the radical blue of a radical sky
he sat radically down in the radical sunshine
with the radical far glimpse of the radical sea
in the radical good weather over radical farmland
where the monetised farmers in their nitrogen-sown fields
with their petrol-driven harvesters and their petrol-driven tractors
mechanically gathered in their final commercial harvest
meanwhile a radical horse on the radical steep ground
of the radical barren slope cropped radical grass
and for a radical hour standing radically still
gazed oot awa into the radical far hyne

Colin Donati

Contributors

Donald Adamson writes in English and Scots, and translates from Finnish. He has been a prize-winner in many competitions, including first prize in the Herald Millenium Competition and the Sangschaw Translation Competition. His latest pamphlet, *All Coming Back* (Roncadora, 2019), takes as its theme the third age of life.

Jim Aitken is a poet and dramatist. His last poetry collection, *Flutterings*, came out in 2016. His poems have appeared in a number of anthologies. He also tutors in Scottish Cultural Studies with Adult Education in Edinburgh and, as well as organising Literary walks around the city, he also tutors with the City's Outlook Programme for people with mental health issues. In 2019 he edited a collection of their poems and prose called *Creative Outlooks*, published by City of Edinburgh Council.

Kate Armstrong is a poet and translator who writes in Scots and English. Her most recent and extensive work was published in *A Kist o Skinklan Things* (ASLS, 2017). She prefers poetry that is read aloud and loves the work of the Northern poets Hadfield, Watt and Jamieson. She lives in Dundee.

Meg Bateman is a Gaelic academic at Sabhal Mòr Ostaig in Skye, part of the University of the Highlands and Islands. Her poetry collections are *Òrain Ghaoil/Amhráin Ghrá*, 1989. *Aotromachd/Lightness*, 1997, *Soirbheas/Fair Wind*, 2007, and *Transparencies*, 2013. She has co-edited and translated four anthologies of historical Gaelic verse.

Henry Bell lives on the Southside of Glasgow and edits Gutter magazine. He is the author of the biography *John MacLean: Hero of Red Clydeside*, and editor of books including *A Bird is not a Stone*, an anthology of Palestinian poetry. In 2019 he won a Scottish New Writers Award for poetry.

Lesley Benzie is originally from Aberdeen but now lives in Kirriemuir, having worked and raised her family in Glasgow for 25 years. She has had her work published in a number of magazines and anthologies. Her first collection *Sewn Up* was followed by a second collection called *Fessen/Reared* which combined both Aberdonian and English.

David Betteridge worked as a teacher and teacher-trainer in several countries, latterly as Head Teacher of Pollockshields Primary School. He also taught at Jordanhill College of Education in Glasgow where he lives. He published

Granny Albyn's Complaint (Smokestack Books, 2008) and edited *A Rose Loupt Oot* (Smokestack Books, 2011), commemorating the UCS Work-In in poetry and song. With designer Tom Malone he has produced a dozen poetry pamphlets under the Rhizome banner.

Chris Boyland lives near Glasgow. His poems have appeared in *404Ink*, *Gutter* and *New Writing Scotland* as well as other magazines and anthologies. His debut pamphlet *User Stories* will be published by Stewed Rhubarb Press in 2020. He is a member of the Scottish Poetry Library's Advisory Group.

Mazigh Buzakhar is a poet originally from native Berbers in North Africa. He writes in Amizigh/Berber and in English. He is fascinated with Amizigh oral literature (Tales, Folk, Proverbs) and is working to have much of these forgotten memories which affirm Berber identity documented. His English poems were published in *Qmunicate, York-Juba Anthology*. He lives in Inverurie.

Bee Parkinson-Cameron's work includes poetry in collections of poetry and prose in *Love, War, Travel, Happy, 'the challenges of finding love', 'uncovered voices' anthology, 'suicide' anthology* and issues 2,3 and 5 of *The Writer's Magazine*. Bee's theatrical organisation was shortlisted for Epic Awards in 2019. She was also longlisted for the 2019 Poetrygram Prize.

George Colkitto writes for the pleasure of words and from the need to describe what he sees and fells. He has poems in Linwood, Johnstone and Erskine Health Centres. He has had two poetry collections published by Diehard Press and Cinnamon Press.

David Cameron was born in Glasgow. In 2014 he received the Hennessy Literary Award for Poetry. His poetry is collected in *The Bright Tethers: Poems 1988-2016*, and his most recent publications are *Samuel Beckett: The Middle and Later Years* and the experimental novel *Prendergast's Fall*.

Nicole Carter is a qualified personal trainer, fitness class instructor and nutrition adviser. She has self-published two poetry collections and had her audio poem *The Shingle Shore* featured in a Poetry Jukebox which toured Northern Ireland. She recites her poetry at gigs and co-manages 3C's Open Mic.

Anne Connolly is an Irish poet settled in Scotland. A former Chair and Makar of the Federation of Writers (Scotland), she has appeared at numerous Festivals including StAnza. She believes that Poetry is music in its own right. *Once upon a Quark* (2019), her third collection, was described by Christine

De Luca as 'funny, pithy, profound.'

A C Clarke lives in Glasgow. Her fifth collection is *A Troubling Woman*. She was a winner in the Cinnamon 2017 pamphlet competition with 'War Baby'. *Druchaid*, with Maggie Rabatski and Sheila Templeton was published by Tapsalteerie last year. She is working on poems about Gala Élouard/Dali and her circle.

Julian Colton has had five collections of poetry published including *Everyman Street* (Smokestack Books), *Cold Light of Morning* (Cultured Llama), and *Two Che Guevaras* (Scottish Borders Council). He edits *The Eildon Tree* literary magazine and contributes articles and reviews. He lives in Selkirk in the Scottish Borders.

Gordon Dargie grew up in Lanarkshire but has lived in Shetland since 1980. He is widowed with two grown-up children. Now retired, he was an English teacher and became Principal of Shetland College. In 2009 Kettillonia published his first collection *a tunnel of love*.

Colin Donati is a Scottish poet who lives somewhat precariously in Edinburgh. He is a regular performer of his work and has published collections with Kettillonia and Red Squirrel Press. He is also a translator of Dostoevsky into Scots and editor of the collected plays of Robert McLellan, *Robert McLellan, Playing Scotland's Story* (Luath, 2014).

Jim Ferguson lives and writes in Glasgow. His research on Paisley poet Robert Tannahill (1774-1810) includes *A Weaver in Wartime, Tannahill and Irish Song*; and *Radicalism in the Work of Robert Tannahill*, which can be found online. Ferguson's other books include *Poor Wurld* (Speculative Books, 2020). Jim's website is www.jimfergusonpoet.co.uk

Alistair Findlay is a poet and editor and author of *Dancing with Big Eunice* and *Mollycoddling the Feckless*. With Tessa Ransford he co-edited *Scotia Nova: Poems for the Early Days of a Better Nation* (Luath Press, 2016). *Lenin's Gramophone: Scotland's Left Poetry and Song 1865-2000* is to be published by Luath Press.

Anne C Frater/ Anna c Frater was brought up in the village of Upper Bayble in the Isle of Lewis, in a home and a community where Gaelic was the main language. Her work has been published in various anthologies, as well as her collections *Fon t-Slige* and *Cridhe Creige*.

Owen Gallagher was born of Irish parents in the Gorbals area of Glasgow. His most recent poetry collection is *Clydebuilt*, published by Smokestack Books, 2019.

Magi Gibson's sixth poetry collection *I Like Your Hat* will be published this year. She won the Scotland on Sunday/Women 2000 Poetry Prize and has held three Scottish Arts Council Writing Fellowships. She has been a Royal Literary Fund Fellow and Writer in Residence in Glasgow's Gallery of Modern Art. She has had many poems published in anthologies, including *Modern Scottish Women Poets* and *Scottish Love Poems*, both published by Canongate. She co-edits *The Poet's Republic*.

Peter Godfrey works as a freelance journalist and lives in the Hebrides, but regularly travels by boat to Latin America, a continent in which he has a special interest. However, his passion is for real writing and he is currently putting together a first poetry collection.

Geraldine Gould, born in Glasgow, is a poet and short story writer who was also an active trade unionist both locally and nationally with the EIS. She holds a Master's Degree in Creative Writing from the University of Dundee where she also contributes to the University's Review of the Arts. She is currently putting together a short story collection on the lives of older women who are too often forcibly retreated from view.

Mandy Haggith won the Robin Jenkins Literary Award in 2009 and is currently poet in residence at Inverewe Gardens. Her books include four poetry collections—*letting light in, Castings, A-B-Tree, Why the Sky is Far Away*—a poetry anthology *Into the Forest*, a non-fiction book, *Paper Trails*, and five novels, *The Last Bear, Bear Witness, The Walrus Mutterer, The Amber Seeker* and the *Lyre Dancers*. She lives on a wooded croft in Assynt and teaches Literature and Creative Writing at the University of the Highlands and Islands.

William Hershaw is a poet, playwright, folk musician and Scots language activist. His *Stars Are The Aizles—Selected Poems in Scots 1976-2016* was published in 2017 by The Neepheid Press. He is the founder of *The Bowhill Players*, a musical and dramatic group who perform the works of Joe Corrie and other Fife based miner poets. In 2018 Grace Note Publications published *The Sair Road*, a Scots version of the Stations of the Cross that is set in the Fife coalfield in the twentieth century. Jim Aitken has written a review/essay of *The Sair Road* for **Culture Matters**.

Tom Hubbard is a novelist, poet and semi-retired academic. His next book, *The Devil and Michael Scot*, will appear from Grace Note Publications in 2020, and a pamphlet shared with Aberdeen City Makar Sheena Blackhall, *Not My Circus Not My Monkey*, will also be published later this year by Malfranteaux Concepts.

Ghazi Hussein is a Palestinian poet and dramatist. His plays include *Jasmine Road* and *One Hour Before Sunrise* and he wrote the script for the film *Trouble Sleeping* (2008), directed by Eunice Olumide and Robert Rae. He reads his poetry at many events throughout Scotland and is currently working on a new play, *Nobody Wants Me*.

Brian Johnstone's poems have appeared in Scotland and over 20 countries worldwide. He has published seven poetry collections, plus a memoir *Double Exposure* (Saraband, 2017). His pamphlet *Juke Box Jeopardy* (Red Squirrel, 2018) was shortlisted for the MacDonald Award 2019. He is a founder and former Director of the StAnza Festival. www.brianjohnstonepoet.co.uk

Vivien Jones lives on the north Solway shore in Scotland. She has two poetry collections and two short story collections in print, numerous inclusions in national and international anthologies, and has work broadcast on Radio Scotland and Radio 4. Recently she has been writing short plays—for which she won a national award—working with actors and directors to bring them to performance. She is one of three editors of *Southlight* literary magazine, based in the south-west of Scotland. She is literature ambassador for the Wigtown Book Festival and often organises creative writing workshops in museums and galleries.

Peter Kelly's poetry has been published online, in film poems and print publications including *Laldy, Spinddrift, Poems for Grenfell Tower* and both Dove Tales anthologies, *A Kind of Stupidity* and *Bridges or Walls?* His first collection *Art of Insomnia* has been accepted for publication in 2020.

Kate Lindsay is a poet who writes in Scots and English. In February 2020, after being shortlisted, she had a poem published in an anthology on *Leaving* by Hammond House. In 2019 she won a first and second prize in the Ayrshire Mental Health & Arts Foundation Poetry Competition.

Christine De Luca writes in English and Shetlandic, her mother tongue. She was Edinburgh's Makar from 2014-2017. Besides several children's stories and one novel, she has had seven poetry collections and five bi-lingual volumes published in French, Italian, Icelandic, Norwegian and English. She has participated in many festivals here and abroad and has been involved in numerous translation activities.

Peter Mackay is a writer, lecturer and broadcaster. He has two collections of poems, *Gu Leòr/Galore* (2015) and *Nàdur De/ Some Kind of* (2020). Originally from the Isle of Lewis, he now lives in Edinburgh and works at the University of St Andrews.

Edward Mackinnon, originally from Fife, is now based in England. He has worked as a translator in the Netherlands and in France. He has had four poetry collections published by Shoestring Press in Nottingham, the latest of which is *The Storm Called Progress*, 2018.

Jim Mainland is a poet from Shetland. He has published three slim poetry collections: *A Package of Measures, The League of Nations* and *Fuglicaavie*. He writes in Shetlandic and English.

Mary McCabe's books include fiction: *Everwinding Times* and *Two Closes and a Referendum*, non-fiction *Streets, Schemes and Stages* and faction *Stirring the Dust*. A children's book and several radio plays appeared in German translation. Dozens of her poems and stories in Scots, English and Gaelic have been anthologised. Politically active, she is a member of PEN International.

Annie McCrae grew up in Dumfries and is now based in Edinburgh. She was an EIS school representative and national organiser of her union. A number of her poems were published in the pamphlet *Magistri Pro Pace* (*Teachers for Peace*) in 2008 and she has read her work at anti-war, Palestine Solidarity and International Women's Day events. She has attended writer courses with the Arvon Foundation as well as Poetry in Practice sessions at Edinburgh University and the Scottish Poetry Library.

Callum Macdonald, from Fife, works for a visual impairment charity in Edinburgh. He runs his own blog with writing on politics, travel, sport, as well as poetry. He is interested in Scottish literature and is passionate about social justice.

Beth McDonough was Writer in Residence at Dundee Contemporary Arts; she reviews for *DURA*. *Handfast* (with Ruth Aylett), explored autism, whilst *Aylett* considered dementia. Anthologised widely, McDonough is published in *Agenda, Causeway, Gutter* and elsewhere. *Lamping for Pickled Fish* (4Word) is her first solo pamphlet.

Stuart McHardy is a storyteller, author of thirty odd books (some odder than others), a poet, a musician and a Teaching Fellow at Edinburgh University's Centre for Open Learning. Founder member and past President of the Pictish Arts Society, he was the original Director of the Scots Language Centre in Perth.

Geordie McIntyre is a Glaswegian of Highland and Irish descent. His lifetime involvement in song, ballad and poetry is reflected in his singing, collecting and song-writing. His early years as a radio and television technician and later as a Modern Studies teacher, coupled with his passion for the outdoors, have in diverse ways fuelled and complemented his prime interest in folk music.

Cara L McKee lives on the West Coast of Scotland and currently still has a job in her local library. Her poetry has been published in various places including *Gutter, The Interpreter's House, Dodging the Rain, Eye Flash Poetry*. Her first pamphlet comes out in 2020 from Maytree Press.

John McMahon is a writer from Dumbarton. He wishes Scotland to grow and prosper for his daughter and her children and to see this nation as an independent one among the family of nations.

Hugh McMillan's work has been published widely in Scotland and beyond in book and pamphlet form. In 2018 the collections *Heliopolis* and *The Conversation of Sheep*, the latter in collaboration with a local shepherd, were published by Luath Press.

Chad Norman lives and writes in Nova Scotia. His Scottish roots are on his mother's side through McKinleys and Grants. He read his work in Glasgow in the Autumn of 2018 at NUI and Over the Edge reading series. His poems have appeared in a number of magazines including *Dreich* and *Chapman*.

Jean Rafferty's latest novel, *Foul Deeds Will Rise*, is about Satanist abuse and was published in 2019 by independent Newcastle publisher, Wild Wolf. Formerly an award-winning journalist, Rafferty has explored many literary forms. Her first two works of fiction were both nominated for literary prizes. She also chairs Dove Tales, an association of Artists for Peace, including it in many cultural events and in publishing two anthologies, *A Kind of Stupidity* (2018) and *Bridges or Walls?* (2019).

Mario Relich, who lives in Edinburgh, is a widely-published poet, including poems in *The Herald, Northwords Now*, and *The Antigonish Review*. His collection *Frisky Ducks* (Grace Note Publications) appeared in 2014. He also contributes regularly to Scottish Affairs on cultural topics, and is a Board member of Scottish PEN.

Olive M Ritch is an award-winning poet from Orkney. She now lives and works in Aberdeen and her poems have been published in many literary magazines, anthologies and websites, including *Poetry Review, Agenda, Gutter, New Writing Scotland, The Poetry Cure* and *In Protest: 150 Poems for Human Rights*. She has also broadcast her work on Radio 4. She is currently working on her debut collection and is this year's recipient of the Scottish Book Trust's Next Chapter Award.

Rose Ann Fraser Ritchie has volunteered for writing and spoken word in the communities of Edinburgh for many years. She is the community poet for Our Health for the NHS. She runs 'Life is too short' events every second Wednesday of the month at the Traverse Theatre. She is on the committee of the Federation of Writers (Scotland) and is a Director with the Scottish Writer's Centre, Glasgow.

Louis Rive is a Scottish singer and songwriter based in Barcelona. His work focuses on the inequality of 21st century living, the world of work, and the feeling of national identity in the modern age.

Colin Rutherford is originally from Ecclefechan and has been writing poetry since 2018. Some of his work has been published along with a number of other Glasgow based poets in the pamphlet *Barrington Drive* in 2018.

Chrys Salt's poems have been published and performed internationally. Her poems have also been translated into several languages. Her poem 'The Burning' was selected as one of the best 20 Scottish poems and 'Weaver of Grass' was shortlisted for the Callum Macdonald Award. She was awarded a Writers Bursary and an MBE for services to the Arts.

Finola Scott's poems are widely published including in *New Writing, Gutter, the Honest Ulsterman, Lighthouse* and *Orbis*. In 2019 Red Squirrel published her pamphlet *Much left unsaid*. Tapsalteerie will publish her Scots poems this year. Her work can be read on Facebook at Finola Scott Poems.

Morag Smith was brought up on a council estate in Glasgow. Her short stories and poetry have been published in numerous magazines and anthologies including *New Writing Scotland, Firth Magazine, Gutter* and *The View From Now* (Speculative Books). She is one of the Mirrorball Clydebuilt Apprentice Poets for 2019=20.

Leela Soma was born in Chennai (Madras), India, and now lives in Glasgow. She has published two novels and two collections of poetry. Her poems have been published in *Gutter, The Blue Nib, The Glasgow Review of Books* and many others. She was nominated for the Pushcart Prize 2020. Some of her work reflects her dual heritage of India and Scotland.

Gerda Stevenson is an award-winning writer, actor, director, singer and songwriter. She has worked in theatre, TV, radio, film and opera. Her poetry collection *If This Were Real* (Smokestack Books, 2013) was translated into Italian. She produced a CD of her songs in *Night Touches Day* (Gean Records, 2014), *Inside & Out: the Art of Christian Small* (Scotland Street Press, 2019) and *Edinburgh* (Allan Wright Photographic, 2019). Her poetry collection *Quines: Poems in tribute to women of Scotland* (Luath Press) was first published in 2018 and has been reprinted in 2020. This collection is also being translated into Italian. A review/essay of *Quines*, written by Jim Aitken, can be found on the **Culture Matters** website.

Fiona Stewart is an artist and designer who studied at the Edinburgh College of Art and at the Bristol Old Vic Theatre School. In 2013 she won the Jocelyn Herbert Award for stage design. She works as a theatre designer, scenic artist and fine artist. She produced scenic art work for Wes Anderson's stop animation films *Isle of Dogs* and *Fantastic Mr Fox*. She also worked on Tim Burton's *Frankenweenie* and the John Lewis 2013 Christmas advert *Bear and the Hare* as well as many West End theatre shows in London. She lives in Kent and produces original prints, paintings and illustrations.

Sheila Templeton writes in Scots and English. A triple winner of the McCash Language Poetry Competition, she has also won the Robert McLellan Poetry Competition, the Neil Gunn Writing Competition and been Makar for the Federation of Writers (Scotland). Her latest publications are *Owersettin* (Tapsalteerie Press, 2016), *Gaitherin* (Red Squirrel Press, 2016), *Drochaid* (Tapsalteerie Press, 2019). She is working on a new collection for 2020.

John Tinney is Glaswegian, a Politics graduate and a warehouse worker. He is published in *404 Ink Magazine Issue 6, Razor Cuts VIII* and on several online publications.

D.A. Watson is a novelist and occasional verse writer from the west coast. He is the author of novels *In the Devil's Name, The Wolves of Langabhat* and *Cuttin Heads*, and the epic poems *Tam o'Shatner, The Cravin* and *AAAHHH Zombies*.

Stephen Watt is Dumbarton FC's Poet-in Residence and was Makar for the Federation of Writers (Scotland). He has four published collections: most recently in 2019 with the crime novel in verse, *Fairy Rock*. Stephen has also edited a punk poetry collection *Ashes to Activists* on behalf of the Joe Strummer Foundation.

Acknowledgements

Meg Bateman's poem 'Ìobairt 2001/ Sacrifice 2001' was first published in *Soirbheas/ Fair Wind*, Polygon/Birlinn, 2007. This poem has been slightly altered for this anthology. Her poem 'Iomallachd/Remoteness' was first published in *Aotromachd agus Dàin Eile/ Lightness and other poems*, Polygon 2018.

A version of **David Betteridge**'s poem 'Only in a Commonweal' was first published in *Granny Albyn's Complaint* (Smokestack Books, 2008) and a version of his poem 'Yes' was first published in *Scotia Nova: Poems for the Early Days of a New Nation* (edited by Alistair Findlay and Tessa Ransford, Luath Press, 2016).

Nicole Carter's poem 'He Spoke Lallans' was first published in *The Homeless Diet*, 2018.

George Colkitto's poem 'In a once city of culture do pearls grow' was first published in *Waitin yae Meet wi the Deil*, Diehard Press, 2018.

Anne Connolly's 'Bee Division' was first published in *Not entirely beautiful* (Stewed Rhubarb, 2013)

Owen Gallagher's 'I saw a new world being assembled' was first published in **Culture Matters**, 2015 and 'Blacklist' was first published in the *Morning Star*, 2018.

Magi Gibson's 'The President Visits for a Quick Round' was first published in *Poets' React*, 2019, 'Our Boys' was first published in the *Morning Star*, 2019.

Geraldine Gould's 'Atlantic' was first published in *The London Grip*, 2017.

Mandy Haggith's 'Immigrants' was first published in *I'm Coming With You*, Scottish PEN anthology, 2017.

Brian Johnstone's 'British Bulldogs' was first published in the *New European* in 2017 and 'Safe' was first published in *The Poet's Republic* in 2017.

Peter Mackay's 'Whoso list to hunt' was first published in *Gu Leór/Galore* in 2015 and 'Geographical Exclusions Apply' was first published in *Nàdur De/ Some Kind of* in 2020.

Edward Mackinnon's 'To Sorley Maclean' was first published in *Killing Time in Arcadia* (Shoestring Press, Nottingham, 2017) and 'Unlawful' was first published in *The Storm Called Progress* (Shoestring Press, Nottingham, 2018).

Beth McDonough's 'The Insecurity of *Margaritifera Margaritifera*' was first published in *Well, Dam* (Beautiful Dragons Collaborations, 2019).

Leela Soma's 'Just Things' was first published in *The Blue Nib 37*, and 'The Laundrette' was first published in *High Tide*, anthology of the Federation of Writers (Scotland), 2019.

D. A. Watson's 'Wasted' was first published in the collection *Tales of What the Fuck*, Wild Wolf Publishing, 2019.

CULTURE MATTERS

Culture Matters is a registered Co-Operative, which aims to promote a progressive political approach to the arts and all other cultural activities.

We believe that culture should be for the many, not the few, and that class-based divisions in society constrain, prevent and spoil our enjoyment of all the cultural activities which we need to enjoy life and be fully human.

We have developed a number of operations to meet our objectives. They include

—a web platform, **www.culturematters.org.uk**, which publishes creative and critical material such as articles, poems, essays and images

—a publishing operation, which publishes poetry and other material as books and ebooks.

Recent Publications

Here is a selection of recent titles, all available to buy online at
www.culturematters.org.uk

Almarks: an anthology of radical poetry from Shetland
edited by Jim Mainland and Mark Ryan Smith

The poems in this anthology are radical in different ways. All broadly strike an attitude; some are explicitly political in content, while others are more indirectly observational and personal. Some are radical in style and approach, such as in their use of Shetland dialect. They all ignore or break boundaries, and so are like almarks—the Scots word for sheep that jump over or break through fences and walls. They are thrawn, awkward, headstrong and independent.

Release a Rage of Red:
The Bread and Roses Poetry Award Anthology 2019
edited by Mike Quille

Release a Rage of Red is a selection of entries to the **Culture Matters** Bread & Roses Poetry Award 2019, including the five winners.

Witches, Warriors, Workers:
An anthology of contemporary working women's poetry
edited by Jane Burn and Fran Lock

This anthology focuses on themes which reflect the texture and preoccupations of working women in contemporary Britain. It contains poems, lyric essays and artwork which explore women's complex relationship to work, to the environment, to families, to their bodies, and to each other.

Living as a woman is a struggle under the multiple oppressions of late-stage capitalism. This anthology addresses such anxieties through poetry and art, while striving to uncover the hidden affinities that exist across different lives, offering an inclusive vision of feminism that is porous, egalitarian, and mutually responsible.

The Children of the Nation:
An anthology of working people's poetry from contemporary Ireland
edited by Jenny Farrell

This is an anthology of poetry in both Irish and English by 67 working-class writers from the thirty-two counties of Ireland. The common focus is on themes which reflect the texture and preoccupations of working-class life in contemporary Ireland. It has been generously supported by the Irish Trade Union movement.

This is the first anthology to be published in Ireland which focuses on poetry written by and about working people and their experiences, cares and concerns. It is inclusive and egalitarian, and values authenticity, relevance and communicativeness as well as literary skill and inventiveness. It is grounded in individual effort, but has transformed these individual endeavours into a collective expression of the lives, aspirations, concerns and hopes of that class in our society which constantly has to struggle to get its voice heard and valued.

Raptures and Captures by Fran Lock, with images by Steev Burgess

Raptures and Captures follows on from **Muses and Bruises** and **Ruses and Fuses**, both published by **Culture Matters**. It is inspired by liberation theology and a fascination with the continuing relevance of the lives of the saints to a radical, liberating politics. As one poem's title states, we are 'In Need of Saints'.

The images by Steev Burgess which accompany the poems share and express the same dialectical combination of anger and gentleness, strength and vulnerability. As in the other two volumes, the stunning, taboo-busting collages poignantly combine the grime and glitter of modern life in fragmented, uncertain but coherent juxtapositions of images and words, reinforcing, developing and extending the meanings of the poems.

Onward / Ymlaen!
An anthology of radical poetry from contemporary Wales
edited by Mike Jenkins

Onward / Ymlaen! is an anthology of poetry in both Welsh and English by around 70 Welsh working-class writers. Gustavius Payne, a well-known Welsh artist, has provided stunningly appropriate paintings to accompany some of the poems in the book. The poems cover a diverse range of political themes and issues including poverty and class inequality, self-determination, internationalism, war, living on a council estate in Swansea, and the death of Jo Cox.

This anthology brings together the finest radical political poetry from contemporary Cymru, reflecting the importance of community, co-operation and commitment to building a better world.

Robots Have No Bones by Fred Voss

Robots Have No Bones is Fred Voss's follow-up collection to **The Earth and the Stars in the Palm of Your Hand**, also published by **Culture Matters**.

In a series of sympathetic, sometimes visionary poems, Voss takes us into the lives of the American working class, manual workers who have been betrayed by successive politicians. Technological advances like robots mean that that there is enough wealth being created for working people not to have to work so hard, for so long, and for so little—but capitalism makes that impossible.

Like the machine presses he writes about, Voss's poems stamp in our minds the nature of capitalist work, and the way it dehumanizes us. They also remind us of the potentially revolutionary strength of working-class people, who remain undefeated in the fight with oppressive bosses, venal politicians, and the financial class whose avarice is as automatic, ingrained and inhuman as the robots they use to make profits.